THE CHEFS OF CUCINA AMORE™

Credits

THE CHEFS OF CUCINA AMORE PRODUCTION TEAM

Publisher: Greg Sharp

Editor: Chris Rylko

Book and Cover Design: Barbara Schmitt

Food Photography: Christopher Conrad

Cover Photograph: Melanie Blair

Culinary Director: Jenny Steinle

Food Stylist: Christina Nordstrom

Copyeditor: Cynthia Sharp

Promotional Copy: Kathy Hogan

Grateful Acknowledgements

Chief Executive Officer, West 175 Enterprises, Inc.: John McEwen

Chief Operating Officer, West 175 Enterprises, Inc.: Rachael Williams

WEST 175 PUBLISHING
POST OFFICE BOX 84848
SEATTLE, WASHINGTON 98124
www.cucinaamore.com

THE CHEFS OF CUCINA AMORE

FOREWORD AND ESSAYS BY

Vincent Schiavelli

RECIPES BY

Nancy Harmon Jenkins, Nick Malgieri, Joe Simone and Faith Willinger

West 175 Publishing

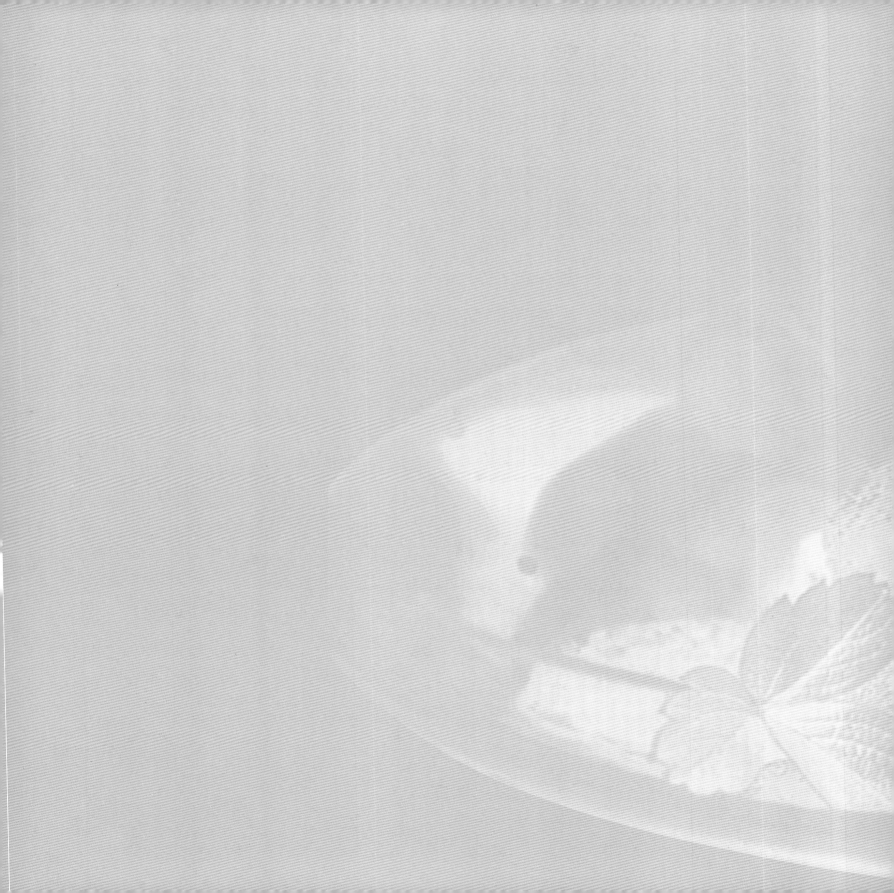

Table of Contents

FOREWORD BY

Vincent
Schiavelli

WHEN I WAS ASKED to host *The Chefs of Cucina Amore*, I was enthralled by the prospect of working with four masters of the Italian kitchen. What I hadn't considered, however, is that I would be actually eating their food—and that has turned out to be the best part of all!

The first day of taping finally arrived. In addition to the crew's work, moving equipment, placing lights and cameras, and all the other bustle of the first day, chefs were checking ingredients and organizing them for the recipes of the day. Our brief, first introductions were filled with phrases like, "Nice to meet you. Could you please pass me that onion?"

In short order, the lights perfectly illuminated the kitchen, and camera operators stood in place behind their enormous, monster-like apparatus. The chefs and I were put in makeup and wired with microphones, and the food ingredients were all in place. The floor director yelled, "Okay everybody, places for the first recipe," and so it began.

After we had taped my short introduction to the show, I joined Nancy Harmon Jenkins in the kitchen for her first recipe. Nancy is a brilliant woman, extremely knowledgeable of the various cuisines of the Mediterranean. She has written several books on food, and innumerable

articles for magazines and newspapers. Born and raised in

Maine, she now lives part of the year in Tuscany. When I asked

why "a nice girl from Maine" was living in Italy, she told me a

most remarkable story.

One day, during her first visit to Rome, she was sitting

in her usual lunch-time trattoria. At the next table sat a Roman gentleman about to eat a peach.

He took it in his hands and rubbed the surface of the peach with the edge of a spoon.

He then peeled off the loosened skin with his fingers and ate the peach with a knife

and fork. Noticing her staring at this unusual but efficient procedure, he said, "We

may have lost the war, but we still know how to peel a peach." Nancy said that from

this moment, she knew that Italy would one day be her home, and that food is "the

quickest way to get inside a culture."

Nancy's food is filled with delicious history and culture that only years of living

all over the world can teach. Her deep understanding that much of the food from

each Mediterranean culture shares basic, common roots has been the inspiration for

many of her wonderful recipes in this book. Her ability to make this culinary history

come alive in our pots and on our tables is the magic of her finely tuned craft.

The ease with which this magic is accomplished is best described in the segment

in which she prepared *Toasted Hazelnut Goat Cheese with Honey-Orange Sauce.* When

she listed the ingredients, I quipped, "What could be more simple?" Her response

came quick and sure: "Fasting."

Joe Simone bounded into the kitchen with the energy of a whirling dervish. The only restaurant chef on the show, it takes just that kind of energy to produce four hundred meals in an evening. For years he was the chef at Tosca in suburban Boston, where he and his partners created an exciting destination restaurant with a national reputation. Joe next came to Cucina Amore, setting it ablaze with hearty, rustic flavors, and we will never be the same.

Before taping, Joe personally chose the various styles and patterns of the platters and bowls on which he would display each finished dish. He very carefully

prepared his *mise en place*, checking and re-checking the ingredients' weight or volume with the exactness of the mathematics major he once was at Brown University. From the moment he stepped into the kitchen, however, Joe's gusto could not be suppressed, and food excitedly flew around the room.

I quickly learned that whenever Joe was going to demonstrate finishing a pasta dish in a skillet, my job was to stand back. I began to think that it was not he who was causing the bits of tomato or onion to fly out of the pan, but the food itself, so brimming over with flavor.

Tasting the savory goodness of Joe's food was the prize after each of his segments. He

made certain that all the crew had as much as they wanted. One time, there was just enough pasta for a small taste. Joe, between segments, cooked up another batch, so everyone would be satisfied. He then went on to cook his recipes for camera the rest of the day. That evening, he invited me to his

brother's home, where he was cooking, "just a small family dinner."
Joe never stops, and the flavors of his food never fail.

Although we had seen each other over the years at food-writers'
conferences, Faith Willinger and I had never actually met. When we were
introduced at Cucina Amore, Faith extended her hand and took a step
forward. I followed suit, and it felt as if we had known each other forever.
From that moment our culinary love affair began.

Faith has lived in Italy for the past twenty-seven years, spending
most of that time in Florence. Her life is engaged with her family and her
work. She has learned and understands better than many native-born
Italians do the deep and subtle mysteries of Italian cuisine, tasting this
food with her heart.

The recipes Faith chose for Cucina Amore are mostly Tuscan. They
are simple and exquisite, depending in large part on the quality of their
ingredients. Even for a television show, Faith could only use the finest.

Cooking on television is a bit like ventriloquism on the radio. For
example, one can say that a certain cruet contains the finest balsamic vinegar, but in reality, the
liquid could be composed of colored water and cornstarch. Since the audience is not there to
taste it, who would know the difference? Being the food lovers we are at Cucina Amore, this
kind of subterfuge is beyond our imagination, and the ingredients, however arcane, are always
what we say they are.

My fondest memory of Faith's true mastery occurred one day while we were waiting for the cameras to be ready. It was just before lunch and we were all a bit peckish. Faith cleaved chunks of Parmigiano reggiano onto a platter, drizzled it with the thick, syrupy contents of a tiny bottle of real, well-aged balsamic vinegar, and served it to us with good, crusty bread. It turns out she never leaves home without her balsamic vinegar stash. It was sublime!

Nick Malgieri's reputation arrived at Cucina Amore long before he did. He is the author of brilliant books on pastry and desserts. His resume reads like a national list of top restaurants. Added to his well-known teaching credentials, these factors served to peak our excitement even more. Perhaps the most experienced and respected baking professional in this country, we awaited his advent with near-religious vigilance.

From the first moment he began cooking, we all became entranced by Nick's hands at work. These are not large hands, although strong and steady. The fingers are defined in fleshy, looping sections with deft, well-trained muscles beneath. The nimble delicacy with which they performed the tasks of mixing or forming the dough showed the expert, refined skill of a true master.

The authentically Italian flavors of Nick's sweet and savory pastries and baked goods are majestic. His *Pasta Frolla*, the crumbly pastry that is the basis for many Italian desserts, is outstanding. Its flavor and texture have just

the right richness and sweetness to complement a wide range of fillings, from a classical ricotta and rice, to a more ancient one of honey and almonds. His calzone transport me to a street corner in Naples, and his cannoli beam me up to a mountain top in Sicily. The best part of all is that his recipes and methods provide sure and easy preparation of these treasures.

It has been a special honor for me to stand beside Nick at the pastry board. The wealth of knowledge I learned from him about the fine art of pastry making has been a gift of immeasurable value.

Over the years of my involvement in the food world, I have encountered a variety of professionals with a variety of personalities. I have met the true masters and the stars-du-jour; those who understand that our first homage is always to the food, and those whose egos push them in front of the dish; the regular folks, from whom I would eat anything they prepared, and the food snobs for whom I resist even opening my mouth to speak, let alone eat. There are people whose food I'm mad about, and people whose food makes me mad. The playing field is vast and the players are international.

I have learned that there is one thing that joins all we "foodies" together. In one tone or another, all of us are saying the same thing: "Please take my recipe and cook it for your family and friends, and bring them together around the table."

Although a basic, human social expression, eating together is a most intimate contract. When we group at the table, we agree that we will open our mouths and put the prepared food inside our bodies. In this exchange, we expect to be nourished and satisfied. The safety

of the dining experience also creates a forum of another kind—a forum for conversation.
It is well documented that every member of a multi-generational family that regularly eats
together benefits from the experience. Children learn from their grandparents the knowledge
of years, and from their parents information about the marketplace. The older generations gain
a better understanding of modern-day youth, feeling more in step with the times. It seems that
even the remembrance of past family dinners can provide a sense of well-being and peace.

The pages that follow are filled with recipes that are sure to delight family and friends alike. Most of them are simple; all are absolutely delicious. I am told that while preparing this food for the photos, the kitchen staff was over-joyed by the ease of preparation and the great tastes these recipes produce.

I am sure that the food of *The Chefs of Cucina Amore*, "love kitchen," will become longed for favorites in your household as they quickly became in mine. And in years to come, when the pages of this book are dog-eared and spotted with olive oil, turning through them will be like reviewing an album of your fondest memories.

Tanti beddi cosi,

(Many beautiful things)

Vincent Schiavelli

NANCY HARMON JENKINS is a nationally acclaimed food writer and an expert in the art of Mediterranean cooking. From her travels throughout the world, Nancy has discovered the dramatic connection between people and their food and divulges her findings in a collection of popular cookbooks including *Mediterranean Diet*. Nancy is consulting editor for *Food and Wine Magazine* and a former staff writer for *The New York Times* Food Section. She also finds time to teach Masters classes at the top cooking schools in the

Nancy Harmon Jenkins

United States and Italy. Nancy has lived, worked, traveled, and raised two children throughout the countries of the Mediterranean making her home in Spain, France, Italy, Lebanon, and Cyprus as well as Hong Kong and England. She currently divides her life between a Tuscan farmhouse and a home on the coast of Maine.

Recipes by Nancy Harmon Jenkins

NICK MALGIERI is well known for his many award-winning cookbooks including *Chocolate: From Simple Cookies to Extravagant Showstoppers* and *Great Italian Desserts*. His recipes have been featured on network television programs and published in the food columns of nearly every major magazine and newspaper. A graduate of the Culinary Institute of America, Nick apprenticed in Switzerland, and later worked in some of the world's most prestigious pastry kitchens, including the Hotel de Paris in Monte Carlo and the Waldorf Astoria in New York. He has spent extensive time in Italy researching techniques and recipes for pastries and desserts. Currently the director of the baking program at the prestigious Peter Kump's New York Cooking School, Nick frequently visits other culinary schools throughout North America sharing his expertise and influencing chefs around the globe.

Nick Malgieri

Recipes by Nick Malgieri

JOE SIMONE is a master of Italian dinners. As a recognized Executive Chef, Joe is a prominent figure in New England's restaurant scene, working at such celebrated restaurants as Boston's Tosca, Al Forno, Topper's at the Wawinet Inn, and the Papa-Razzi collection of 14 restaurants. Joe has studied the authentic secrets of European cuisine first hand in Greece,

France, and Italy. He is famous for combining the essence of Italian cooking with American tastes. Between commitments as a chef in high demand, Joe joins Faith Willinger in leading culinary tours throughout Europe.

Joe Simone

Recipes by Joe Simone

FAITH WILLINGER is an Italian food scholar trained by the most celebrated chefs in Florence, Rome, and Tuscany. She has spent more than three decades diligently studying Italian cuisine and history while exploring every region in search of exotic menus. She has shared her passion for fresh and seasonal ingredients in her award-winning cookbooks, *Red, White & Greens* and *Eating in Italy*. Faith is recognized as an American expert who understands the deep and subtle mysteries of Italian cuisine and tastes the food with her heart. She and her husband, Massimo, spend most of their time in Florence.

Faith Willinger

Recipes by Faith Willinger

CHAPTER
ONE

Appetizers & Salads

IN ITALIAN, *PASTO* means "the meal," which officially begins with the *primo piatto*, the first course. So the appetizer, or anti-pasto is something eaten outside (anti) the meal, before the first course. Logical, if somewhat convoluted.

An appetizer's purpose is to subtly open one's appetite for the delicious melody of courses to follow. To achieve this end, Italian appetizers often contain vinegar or lemon juice, or are composed of vegetables and other ingredients with sharp or tangy flavors.

These "appetite undressers," the literal translation of the Sicilian term for appetizers, can also be used for other dining purposes. The *Asparagus Frittata with Parmesan and Mint* and the *Three Onion Tart*, for example, can be served as luncheon or as light second courses.

Asparagus Frittata with Parmesan and Mint

EGGS PLAY AN IMPORTANT

culinary role all over the Mediterranean region. This is an example of a frittata—a simple quiche if you will. It makes a wonderful light lunch when paired with a salad. I love the combination of asparagus, mint and Parmigiano cheese. In fact, each spring when the local asparagus makes its brief appearance at our markets here in Boston, I satisfy my craving and really indulge in perhaps too much asparagus. Do not be afraid to serve the frittata at room temperature! Simply cook and eat it within four hours.

joe simone

SERVES 4 TO 6

1 pound (450 g) asparagus, ends trimmed and discarded
8 eggs
1¼ tablespoons extra-virgin olive oil

½ cup loosely packed, chopped fresh mint leaves
¼ cup freshly grated Parmigiano Reggiano cheese or to taste
Kosher or sea salt to taste

METHOD   Bring a large pot of cold water to the boil. Add a generous pinch of salt and the asparagus and blanch for 1-2 minutes or until the bases are tender. Drain immediately and refresh under cold running water. Dry well with paper towel. This can be done one day ahead. Simply cover the blanched asparagus with plastic wrap and store in the refrigerator until ready to continue.

Preheat the oven to 325°F (170°C). Crack the eggs into a large non-reactive bowl and season with a pinch of salt. Whisk until the eggs are light and fluffy, about 3 minutes.

Cut the blanched asparagus into ¼ inch (6 mm) pieces. Warm the olive oil in a large ovenproof non-stick skillet. Add the asparagus pieces to the skillet and cook for 2 minutes. Add the mint and cook for 1 minute. Add the eggs and stir with a wooden spatula or heat resistant rubber spatula as if you were making scrambled eggs. Continue stirring and cooking over medium-low heat until the eggs are about halfway set. Stir in the Parmigiano. Place the pan into the preheated oven and bake until the frittata is lightly set, about 8 minutes. Do not overcook. Remove the frittata from the oven and let cool at least 10 minutes before serving.

Serve warm or at room temperature.

HINT   If you do not have an ovenproof skillet you can begin the recipe on top of the stove and finish baking the frittata in a small baking pan which has been rubbed with a tiny amount of additional olive oil.

Asparagus Frittata with Parmesan and Mint

Crispy Polenta with Greens and Goat Cheese

SERVES 4 TO 6

The Crispy Polenta

1 cup cornmeal, preferably Gray's stoneground coarse

3 - 3½ cups cold water

1 teaspoon salt

1 tablespoon extra-virgin olive oil

2 tablespoons chopped fresh herbs, such as Italian parsley, chives, or oregano

1 tablespoon unsalted butter

¼ cup freshly grated Parmigiano Reggiano cheese

The Greens and Goat Cheese

2-3 cups mesclun, or other greens

2 tablespoons extra-virgin olive oil

1½ teaspoons aged balsamic vinegar

½ cup crumbled goat cheese or to taste

Kosher or sea salt and freshly ground black pepper to taste

METHOD For the crispy polenta, in a medium non-reactive saucepan, bring the cold water to a boil. Whisk in the cornmeal and immediately reduce the heat to low. Simmer very slowly for about 20 minutes, stirring often, until the cornmeal has absorbed almost all of the water and is tender. Stir in the herbs, butter and cheese and cook, stirring, until the ingredients are incorporated and the mixture is creamy. Remove from the heat and check for salt. Pour into a 9 x 9 inch (23 x 23 cm) pan and let cool completely, preferably overnight in the refrigerator.

Just before serving, preheat the oven to 450°F (230°C). Lightly brush a baking sheet with olive oil. Score the cooled polenta in the pan into squares, triangles or any shape. Using a spatula, carefully remove the shapes and invert onto the prepared pan. Brush the exposed edges of the polenta with olive oil and roast for 10-12 minutes until the polenta is beginning to crisp. Flip the polenta pieces over and roast for 6-8 minutes until the polenta is very crisp. Remove the polenta from the oven and transfer to individual serving plates.

For the greens and goat cheese, in a large bowl toss all the ingredients except the goat cheese until well mixed. Divide the tossed salad on top of the polenta. Sprinkle the goat cheese over the salad and serve.

HINTS I never toss the salad until the polenta is just out of the oven.

Also, the amount of water will vary depending on the age and grind of the polenta. The older and coarser the polenta, the more water you will need.

THIS IS A DELICIOUS light lunch or first course. You can use leftover soft polenta for this recipe. I love to use organic, stoneground, coarse cornmeal when I prepare polenta. Several of my Italian friends call my cornmeal "birdfeed" but this doesn't sway me! In fact coarse cornmeal is less prone to "clumping." Be sure to purchase the best quality balsamic vinegar you can. No, I am not suggesting the extra *vecchio*, or very old type which will set you back $100 or more for a mere ounce, but do look for artisanally made aceto and try not to use the bland commercial stuff.

joe simone

Crispy Polenta with Greens and Goat Cheese

Fried Beets with Goat Cheese Vinaigrette

to Italy you surely know that the Italians will fry almost anything! Meatballs, fish, artichokes—even the tender blossoms of the zucchini-plant—get crisped in hot oil. Well, in this recipe I extend the frying technique to beets. Now everyone has an opinion about beets: either they love them or cannot stand to be in the same room with them! I can honestly say that I have converted several people to the cause of the lowly beet with this recipe.

joe simone

SERVES 4 TO 6

4 large beets, about 1½ pounds (750 g), preferably gold	12 oil-cured pitted black olives, sliced
¼ cup all-purpose flour	12 cherry tomatoes, cut in half
½ cup seltzer water	1 tablespoon red wine vinegar
Olive, peanut or vegetable oil, to fry the beets	1½ tablespoons extra-virgin olive oil
1 large bunch arugula, washed and cut into thin ribbons	¼ cup goat cheese or more to taste, crumbled
	Kosher or sea salt and black pepper to taste

METHOD   Preheat the oven to 425°F (220°C). Wash the beets and place them in a roasting pan and roast until the outsides are charred and the beets are tender, about 45 minutes, depending on the size of the beets. Remove from the oven and set aside until cool enough to handle. Wearing gloves, peel the beets and cut into half moons about ⅓ inch (7 mm) thick. This can be done the night before serving: simply cover the beets and store in the refrigerator until ready to proceed.

In a small bowl, make a pastella by whisking together the flour and seltzer. The consistency should be slightly thicker than heavy whipping cream. You may need to add a little extra flour.

In a large fry pan, heat the frying oil to 350°F (180°C). Dip each beet segment into the pastella. The beets should be thinly coated. Carefully slip the coated beets into the oil, without overlap. You may have to fry in batches. Fry the beets until they are golden brown and puffy, about 4 minutes, turning them over once or twice. Remove to a paper towel-lined ovenproof plate and keep warm in a 200°F (100°C) oven until all of the beets are fried.

In a small bowl, toss the arugula, olives, tomatoes and salt, to taste, until well mixed. Add the red wine vinegar, olive oil and goat cheese and toss again.

To serve, arrange the beets on a serving platter, top with the "salad" and serve at once, passing the pepper mill as desired.

HINT   In this recipe the cooked beets are dipped into *pastella* which is an Italian batter made with sparkling water and all-purpose flour. Be sure to use a water with a very mild flavor. Waters that are high in minerals will not do well here.

Fried Beets with Goat Cheese Vinaigrette

Grilled Ratatouille

SERVES 4 TO 6

1 large eggplant

3 large sweet bell peppers, red, yellow,
    or a combination

1 whole salted anchovy or 2 canned
    anchovy fillets

3 garlic cloves, chopped

1 cup extra-virgin olive oil

2 red onions, quartered

1 zucchini, cut in half lengthwise

3 ripe but still firm tomatoes, halved

2 tablespoons finely sliced fresh basil
    leaves, for garnish

2 tablespoons capers, rinsed if salted,
    coarsely chopped, for garnish

Sea salt and freshly ground black pepper
    to taste

METHOD   Slice the eggplant into sticks the size of your index finger. Place the pieces in a colander and toss with a tablespoon of salt. Place a plate on top, weight it down and set aside to drain for at least 40 minutes. Rinse thoroughly to remove the salt and dry with paper towels. Set aside.

Light a grill and when it is hot, roast the peppers until the skins are blackened and blistered. (If you must, place them on a baking sheet and roast under a hot electric broiler.) Transfer the blackened peppers to a paper bag and set aside for at least 40 minutes. Remove and rub off the blackened skins. Discard the stems, seeds and ribs. Slice lengthwise into strips about ½ inch (1.5 cm) wide. Transfer the pepper strips to a large serving bowl. Keep the grill hot.

If you're using a salted anchovy, split and debone the fish. Rinse the fillets under running water to remove as much salt as possible. If you're using canned anchovy fillets this is unnecessary. In a small bowl, chop the anchovies and garlic together to make a coarse mixture. Add the olive oil and mix well. Add about ¼ cup of this to the pepper strips and stir until well coated. Drop the rinsed and dried eggplant slices in the flavored oil and leave to marinate while you prepare the remaining vegetables.

Thread the onion quarters onto skewers, brush with a little of the oil marinade and roast on the grill until the outsides are starting to blacken. Remove the onions, chop roughly and add to the peppers in the serving bowl.

continued on following page

THE COMBINATION OF eggplant, peppers and tomatoes can be found all over the Mediterranean, but too often is overcooked to the point that it becomes bland and mushy. Grilling the vegetables, then combining them, solves this problem. You can serve this on its own or as a first course, as an accompaniment to grilled or roasted meat (superb with roast chicken!), or combine it with a short tubular pasta like fusilli (corkscrews) or farfalline (butterflies) for a hearty vegetarian main course.

nancy harmon jenkins

Grilled Ratatouille

continued from previous page

Brush the zucchini halves with a little of the oil marinade and roast them on the grill. When brown, remove and slice about ½ inch (1.5 cm) thick. Add to the peppers and onions and mix well.

Brush the tomato halves with the marinade and place them, cut-side-down, on the grill. When the cut-side is brown, turn and roast them until the skins are blackened and loose. Remove and chop each half into smaller pieces. Scrape the tomatoes, with their juices, into the other vegetables.

Finally, roast the eggplant sticks on the grill until they are well browned on all sides. Remove and add to the other vegetables. Toss all the vegetables together well, adding any remaining marinade along with salt and pepper if necessary. Garnish with the slivered basil and capers.

Grilled Ratatouille may be served immediately or set aside until ready, but should be served at room temperature, not chilled.

Crostini with Long Cooked Zucchini and Eggplant

SERVES 4 TO 6

2 pounds (900 g) zucchini, the smallest
  you can find

2 pounds (900 g) eggplant, preferably Sicilian

1 cup extra-virgin olive oil

½ cup loosely packed, coarsely chopped
  fresh basil leaves

6 slices country-style bread, preferably
  day-old

2 cups ricotta salata or goat cheese,
  crumbled

Kosher or sea salt and freshly ground black
  pepper to taste

METHOD   Place the zucchini in a large bowl filled with ice water for 20 minutes.

While the zucchini are soaking, trim the eggplant and cut into ½ inch (1.5 cm) cubes with the skin on. Pour half of the olive oil into a large skillet over medium-high heat and, when hot, add enough eggplant to cover the bottom of the pan in one layer—do not overcrowd the pan. Cook, stirring often, until the eggplant has wilted and begun to carmelize, about 10 minutes. Using a slotted spoon, transfer to a large non-reactive bowl. Sprinkle with salt to taste and a little of the basil. Repeat with the rest of the eggplant, adding additional olive oil to the pan as needed.

Drain the zucchini and pat it dry with paper towel. Cut the zucchini into ½ inch (1.5 cm) cubes. In the same large skillet, cook the zucchini in the same manner as the eggplant, transferring it to the bowl with the cooked eggplant. When all of the vegetables have been cooked, add any remaining olive oil from the skillet to the cooked vegetables, along with any remaining basil and toss to mix well.

Just before serving, gently warm the zucchini/eggplant mixture.

Preheat the oven broiler. Place the bread on a baking sheet and toast the bread on both sides.

To serve, arrange the bread on a serving platter, top with the warm zucchini/eggplant mixture and sprinkle with the cheese. Serve at once, passing the pepper mill.

HINT   The vegetables can be cooked and tossed with the basil the day ahead. Simply cover and refrigerate until ready to use. Be sure to gently reheat the vegetables before assembling the crostini.

INGREDIENTS TIP   Ricotta salata is a Sicilian cheese that is made from sheep's milk. It is soft, white, mild and rindless.

IN EUROPE VEGETABLES are generally cooked much longer than here in the United States. My Italian grandmother simply refused to eat "crunchy" cooked vegetables and she would demand that I cook her vegetables to her liking! I struggled with the long cooking of vegetables for many years but have come to realize that the flavors you get when you allow the sugars to caramelize and the fibers to break down are ethereal. This crostini is a delicious way to start a summer dinner or a perfect accompaniment to a light salad.

joe simone

Italian Toast: Fettunta, Bruschetta and Variations

MY FAVORITE DISH IN

the world, far easier to

make than the garlic bread

I knew about before I

moved to Italy. In Florence,

where I live, it's called

fettunta, a contraction of

the words "slice" and "oily."

faith willinger

SERVES 1

1 slice rustic country-style bread,
   about ½ inch (1.5 cm) thick
1 garlic clove
2-3 tablespoons extra-virgin olive oil

Optional Toppings:
2-3 tablespoons each of cooked white beans,
   cooked chick-peas, diced tomatoes
   and a little basil
Fine sea salt to taste

METHOD   Toast or grill the bread lightly until the surface has lightly browned and hardened, but do not dry it out. Rub with the garlic clove, peeled or unpeeled. The rough surface of the bread will grate the garlic onto the toast. Place the toast on a serving dish and drizzle generously with the olive oil. Traditional Tuscans dip the bread into an urn or extra-virgin olive oil. Inferior bread or olive oil will yield greasy toast — not a great idea.

    Top the fettunta with white beans, chick-peas, or tomatoes, as desired. Garnish with basil and sprinkle with salt to taste.

HINT   Slightly smash the chick-peas before topping the toast so they don't roll around.

Italian Toast: Fettunta, Bruschetta and Variations

TALEGGIO IS A DESSERT

cheese, often served with

fruit or a glass of fine red

wine, but it makes a rich

sauce for this tart with three

different onions — or rather,

two onions and a leek. The

white onion mentioned here

is the fresh-from-the garden

kind that has not yet formed

a papery skin on the outside.

If you can't find these, a

bunch of green onions or

scallions will do very well.

This tart may also be made

as small tartlets for an hors

d'oeuvre or buffet table, in

which case they will be done

in half the time allotted

above.

nancy harmon jenkins

Three Onion Tart
Torta di Tre Cipolle con Taleggio

SERVES 12 AS AN APPETIZER OR 4 AS A MAIN DISH

For the Tart Crust
¼ teaspoon active dry yeast
Very warm water
1 cup unbleached all-purpose flour, plus
    a little more for kneading
A little extra-virgin olive oil, for the bowl
    and the baking sheet
3-4 tablespoons fine cornmeal
For the Tart Filling
1 fat leek, trimmed and thinly sliced
2 tablespoons extra-virgin olive oil

1 large fresh white onion, if available,
    or 1 bunch scallions, including green tops,
    thinly sliced
1 large red onion, thinly sliced
1 large egg
¼ pound (225 g) creamy taleggio cheese
2 tablespoons cream, if necessary
2 tablespoons freshly grated Parmigiano
    Reggiano cheese
Sea salt and freshly ground black pepper
    to taste

METHOD   For the tart crust, start at least 1¼ hours before serving. In a small bowl, sprinkle the yeast over ¼ cup of very warm water and let sit until dissolved. Add the flour and stir until it forms a soft dough. Add more warm water if needed. Transfer the dough to a lightly floured board and knead for 3-5 minutes, or until you feel the gluten stretching and the dough becomes springy to the touch. Rub a little olive oil around the inside of a large bowl, add the dough to the bowl, cover with plastic and set aside in a warm place to rise for 45 minutes to 1 hour, or until the dough has doubled.

Transfer the risen dough to a lightly floured board. Punch it down and spread it into a rough circle. Sprinkle the cornmeal over the top, roll it up and knead for 5 minutes, until the cornmeal has been thoroughly incorporated. The crust may be made ahead to this point and the dough refrigerated until ready to use. Bring the dough back to room temperature before continuing. Kneading refrigerated dough will help to warm it up.

Lightly oil a baking sheet or a 12 inch (30 cm) tart or pizza pan. Roll the dough into a circle about 12-14 inches (30-35 cm) in diameter and place on the prepared pan. Cover with a dish towel and set aside in a warm place while you make the filling.

Preheat the oven to 425°F (220°C). Combine the olive oil and leeks in a sauté pan over medium-low heat and cook the leeks until they are melted. Do not let them brown. Add the fresh onion or scallions and the red onion, adding another tablespoon or so of olive oil if the mixture seems very dry. Cook, stirring frequently, until the onions are meltingly soft. The entire process may take as much as 45 minutes. Do not let the onions brown. Remove from the heat and set aside.

In a medium bowl, beat the egg briefly. Beat in the taleggio, a little at a time, beating just long enough to mix. If the teleggio is very firm, beat in a tablespoon or two of cream to lighten the mixture. Stir in the cooked onions with their oil. Taste for seasoning, adding salt and pepper if necessary. Spread the mixture into the prepared dough, leaving a ½ inch (1.5 cm) border all around or pour it into the prepared tart pan. Bake in the preheated oven for 10 minutes. Remove from the oven, scatter the grated Parmigiano over the top and return to the oven for 10 minutes. Remove and let cool slightly before serving.

INGREDIENTS TIP   The vegetables for the filling may be changed with the season. In full summer, for instance, a colorful mixture of sweet red and yellow bell peppers could be substituted for the onion mixture.

Composed Salad of Grilled Asparagus, Fennel and Fresh Mozzarella

I HOPE YOU LOVE ASPAR-agus as much as I do. This is a simple salad that you will compose on your serving platter—beautiful in its presentation and delicious in its simplicity. It is important that you shave the fennel as thinly as possible, almost translucent in its thinness. I have even begged the person manning the deli counter at my local supermarket to shave it for me on his extremely clean meat slicer!

joe simone

SERVES 4 TO 6

2 pounds (900 g) asparagus, ends trimmed and discarded

2 balls fresh mozzarella, about ½ pound (225 g)

½ bulb fennel, about ¼ pound (115 g)

½ head radicchio, about 3 ounces (90 g), preferably Treviso

¼ cup loosely packed, coarsely chopped fresh basil leaves

2 tablespoons freshly squeezed lemon juice

6 tablespoons extra-virgin olive oil

Kosher or sea salt to taste

METHOD Preheat a charcoal grill or set your oven to 400°F (200°C). Bring a large pot of cold water to a boil and add a generous pinch of salt. Add the asparagus and blanch until the ends become tender, about 2 minutes. Immediately drain the asparagus and refresh under cold running water. Let drain and dry well with paper towels.

In a large bowl, toss the asparagus with 2 tablespoons of the olive oil and a pinch of salt. Place on a baking sheet and grill or roast until tender and a bit charred, about 5-7 minutes. Remove from the heat and set aside until cool.

Using a mandoline or vegetable peeler, shave the fennel very thinly into a bowl of ice water. Let rest in the ice water for at least 10 minutes until crisp.

Remove the core from the radicchio and cut into very thin strips.

Drain the mozzarella, discarding its brine. Cut the cheese into ¼ inch (6 mm) cubes and place in a large mixing bowl. Drain the fennel well and add to the cheese. Add the basil, radicchio, lemon juice, remaining 4 tablespoons of the olive oil and salt to taste and toss well.

To serve, arrange the asparagus spears on individual serving plates. Divide the fennel salad on top, drizzling any remaining juices from the salad over the asparagus. Pass the pepper mill and enjoy.

HINT Do not refrigerate the asparagus spears once you grill or roast them. You can blanch the asparagus the day before and let them rest on paper toweling, covered with plastic wrap, in your refrigerator and then simply roast them within 3 or 4 hours of serving.

Composed Salad of Grilled Asparagus,
Fennel and Fresh Mozzarella

Pecorino and Fava Bean Salad

SERVES 2

1 pound (450 g) fresh fava beans
4 ounces (125 g) fresh pecorino cheese
Extra-virgin olive oil to taste
Fine sea salt and freshly ground black
    pepper to taste

METHOD   For a traditional serving, place a basket of the unshelled fava beans in their pods on the table along with the sliced, peeled cheese. Diners should shell the fava beans, then eat a bean, then take a bite of the cheese.

Sophisticated cooks will want to shell the fava beans in the kitchen, dice the pecorino cheese, and marinate with the extra-virgin olive oil, salt and pepper.

INGREDIENTS TIP   If fava beans are not available, use fresh peas as a substitute.

AS YOU WILL SEE IN THE recipe, this can be served in two ways: rustic cooks serve pecorino cheese in a hunk with a basket of fresh fava beans, but refined cooks shell the beans, peel and dice the cheese and marinate with extra-virgin olive oil, salt and pepper. If you don't want to serve it as an appetizer, use it after the main dish, as a cheese course.

faith willinger

Pecorino and Fava Bean Salad

Raw Zucchini, Walnut and Parmigiana Salad

THIS TASTY SALAD

can be served as an

appetizer or a side dish.

faith willinger

SERVES 4 TO 6

2 small or 1 medium zucchini

½ cup shelled walnuts

1 tablespoon chopped fresh parsley

3 tablespoons extra-virgin olive oil

1 teaspoon balsamic vinegar (optional)

Fine sea salt and freshly ground black
  pepper to taste

1 (4 ounce) (115 g) piece Parmigiano
  Reggiano cheese

METHOD   Trim the tip (not the stem end) off the zucchini and cut into wafer thin slices. Use a mandoline or by hand with a ¹⁄₁₆ inch (1 mm) food processor blade. Be very careful!

Transfer the zucchini to a medium bowl, add the walnuts, parsley, olive oil, vinegar (if using), sea salt and pepper and mix well. Arrange the mixture on a serving platter. Using a vegetable parer, shave large curls of the cheese directly over the vegetables, covering the entire salad.

Raw Zucchini, Walnut and Parmigiana Salad

CHAPTER TWO

Pasta, Gnocchi & Soups

ITALIANS ARE MAD about soup. Eating it in all seasons, they buy, harvest, or forage ingredients, depending upon seasonal availability. The dried beans and pasta of a winter soup are generally constant, but the fresh vegetables and greens for a spring or summer minestrone can change weekly.

Italians are generous at the table but frugal in the kitchen, wasting nothing. Many of the soups in this chapter find ways to turn stale bread, bits of Parmigiano, and even a lonely egg into dinner. Many of these hearty, warming soups could easily emerge out of a seemingly bare cupboard.

Soup in Italy is usually eaten as a first course, but also finds its place as a light supper or late-night snack. In the United States, where lunch is not the main meal of the day, these soups will suit very well.

It has been said that if Italy has produced nothing else in the past three thousand years, it has nurtured an entire culture of people who can cook a dish of pasta in the dark, blindfolded.

The culinary road that leads to this end has looped thousands of miles over many centuries. Pasta was not brought from China by Marco Polo, as many believe, but, rather, its origins are Persian; Iranians today still eat a rudimentary pasta called *reshte*.

Trade routes brought the pasta-making process to Tunisia, and from there it was introduced into Sicily in the ninth century. Existing to this day in a Sicilian town called Trabia are records of a macaroni factory that pre-date Marco Polo's exploits by more than two hundred years.

Today, all regions of Italy, even individual cities and towns, are known for particular cuts of pasta, designed to enhance the flavorful sauces of traditional dishes. Sometimes these dishes call for homemade, fresh pasta, but mostly the pasta used is store-bought and dried. And Italy has more pasta producers than political parties!

The mystery of determining the quality of the pasta in this box or that package is easy to unravel. Only use product imported from Italy or made by small, gourmet, domestic producers. The ingredients should simply read: 100% durum wheat flour or semolina, and water. The color should be that of straw. Too yellow a color probably means that food coloring has been added to enhance the appearance of poor quality wheat; too pale, and this inferiority is more apparent.

The surface finish should be dull rather than shiny. Gloss on the surface of the pasta means that it has been dried too quickly, impacting the flavor and the ability of the pasta to hold the sauce. The surface texture is best when it is slightly rough, like an emery board. This texture, however, will be found only in the pasta of better quality handmade or artisanal brands.

Water, the only other ingredient, is also important to taste. Generally, pasta from southern Italy or Sicily is made with better water than that from the north. However, if the product is from a small, artisanal producer and the other factors are in place, the water used is sure to be sweet and pure, regardless of region.

In Italy, pasta is eaten as a first course—never as a side dish and rarely as a complete meal. The number of servings per recipe in this chapter reflects this dining concept.

Pasta with Baked Tomato Sauce

THERE'S JUST ONE SECRET

to this simple dish: make sure

the tomatoes are really ripe and

juicy. If cherry tomatoes don't

look great, use any small, red,

ripe tomatoes, cutting them

into quarters if necessary.

nancy harmon jenkins

SERVES 4

⅓ cup extra-virgin olive oil

1 pound (450 g) very ripe cherry tomatoes, halved

⅓ cup plain dried breadcrumbs

2 tablespoons freshly grated pecorino Romano cheese

4 tablespoons freshly grated Parmigiano Reggiano cheese

2 garlic cloves, finely chopped

1 pound (450 g) fusilli (corkscrew) or butterfly (farfalline) pasta

¼ cup loosely packed basil leaves, torn

Sea salt and freshly ground black pepper to taste

METHOD   Preheat the oven to 400°F (200°C). Use one third of the oil to smear over the bottom of a pyrex oven pan. Set the tomatoes in the pan, cut-side-up. There should be just enough to fit comfortably in the dish with no crowding.

In a small bowl, combine the breadcrumbs with the two cheeses and the garlic and toss with a fork to mix well. You may use just Parmigiano Reggiano if you don't have a good pecorino Romano. Sprinkle this over the cherry tomatoes, making sure that each cut-side is well covered with the crumb mixture. Sprinkle with the salt and pepper to taste and place in the preheated oven to roast until the tomatoes are thoroughly cooked and starting to brown on top, about 20 minutes.

While the tomatoes are cooking, bring a large pot of lightly salted water to a rolling boil. Plunge in the pasta and cook for 8-10 minutes, or until it is done to your liking. Time the pasta so it finishes cooking about the time the tomatoes are ready to come out of the oven. (The tomatoes can wait for the pasta, but the pasta can't wait for the tomatoes.)

When the tomatoes are done, pull them out of the oven, add the torn basil leaves and stir vigorously to mix everything into something like a sauce. Drain the pasta and immediately turn it into the hot oven dish, stirring to mix well with the remaining olive oil. Alternatively, you could turn the pasta into a large heated bowl, immediately add the hot tomato mixture and stir until coated well. Serve immediately, but no cheese.

Pasta with Baked Tomato Sauce

Pasta with Speedy Cherry Tomato Sauce

IT SEEMS THAT DECENT

cherry tomatoes, still attached

to the vine, are available for

most of the year. Tomato sauce

has never been so easy.

faith willinger

SERVES 4 TO 6

6 quarts (5.5 l) water
2-3 tablespoons sea salt
½ pound (225 g) spaghetti
2 garlic cloves
⅛ teaspoon dried red pepper flakes
2-3 tablespoons extra-virgin olive oil

½ pound (225 g) cherry tomatoes,
   cut in half or quarters
1 cup reserved pasta cooking water
1-2 tablespoons of the fresh herb of your
   choice: basil, parsley, oregano, or
   arugula—ONLY ONE (optional)

METHOD   In a large pot, bring the water to a rolling boil. Add the salt and spaghetti and cook until quite *al dente* (hard), about ¾ done.

While the pasta is cooking, place the garlic and chili pepper in a large non-stick skillet, drizzle with the oil and place over medium heat until the garlic barely begins to brown. Add the tomatoes, raise the heat to high, and cook until the tomatoes are wilted, about 4-5 minutes. Set aside.

When the pasta is cooked to quite *al dente*, drain well, reserving 1 cup of the starchy pasta cooking water. Add the drained pasta to the sauce in the skillet. Pour in ¼ cup of the pasta cooking water and cook over the highest heat, stirring with a wooden fork to mix the pasta and sauce very well. Add more pasta cooking water if the sauce dries out and the pasta isn't cooked. Sprinkle with the chopped herb before serving, if desired.

Pasta with Garlic and Lemon Zest

SERVES 4

6 quarts (5.5 l) water

2 tablespoons sea salt

1 pound (450 g) spaghetti or linguine

2-3 garlic cloves, minced

4 tablespoons extra-virgin olive oil

1-2 tablespoons chopped fresh Italian parsley, basil, or arugula

2-3 teaspoons minced lemon zest

Freshly ground black pepper to taste

1 cup reserved pasta cooking water

METHOD   In a large stockpot, bring the water to a rolling boil. Add the salt and spaghetti and cook until quite *al dente* (hard), about ¾ done.

While the pasta is cooking, place the garlic in a large skillet, drizzle with the olive oil and cook, over low heat until it barely begins to color. Add the parsley, lemon zest, black pepper to taste and a pinch of the salt, remove the pan from the heat and set aside.

When the pasta is cooked to quite *al dente*, drain well, reserving 1 cup of the starchy pasta cooking water.

Add the drained pasta to the sauce in the skillet. Pour in ¼ cup of the pasta cooking water and cook over the highest heat, stirring with a wooden fork to mix the pasta and sauce. Add more of the pasta cooking water if the sauce dries out and the pasta isn't cooked. The sauce should be slightly soupy.

THIS IS A RECIPE TO make when the cupboard is bare. A fresh herb like parsley, basil or even arugula is a nice touch but can be skipped if you don't have any. Since this recipe has so few ingredients, each of them must be first rate.

faith willinger

Fettuccini with Raw Vegetable Sauce

MY FAVORITE PASTA

recipes tend to be these

quick, last-minute combina-

tions that reinforce my sense

of pasta as the original

(and still the best) fast food.

nancy harmon jenkins

SERVES 4 TO 6

2 very ripe large tomatoes, peeled,
   seeded and finely chopped

¼ cup imported pitted green olives, chopped

2 tablespoons capers, preferably
   salt-cured, chopped

1 tablespoon freshly squeezed lemon juice

2 garlic cloves, finely chopped

¼ cup finely chopped fresh Italian parsley

1 tablespoon finely chopped fresh basil,
   mint, or oregano

4 anchovy fillets, preferably salt-packed,
   chopped

¼ cup extra-virgin olive oil

1 pound (450 g) fettuccine, tagliatelle,
   or linguine pasta

Freshly ground black pepper to taste

METHOD In a large bowl, combine all the ingredients except the pasta and set aside for at least 30 minutes and up to several hours to let the flavors meld. No refrigeration is necessary.

Bring a large pot of lightly salted water to a rolling boil. Add the pasta all at once and stir to make sure it is well distributed through the boiling water. Cook, partially covered, until done to taste.

As soon as the pasta is done, drain it and immediately turn it into the bowl with the sauce. Stir to combine well, adding more black pepper, if you wish. Serve immediately. However, unlike most pasta dishes, this recipe actually holds well for an hour or so before serving. Just make sure it's thoroughly mixed to coat every strand of pasta with the sauce. Cover lightly with a piece of aluminum foil or a kitchen towel and set aside at room temperature until ready to serve.

HINT When the hot pasta meets with the sauce, it will make the tomatoes sweat and the liquid will be a little "soupy." It will thicken up and absorb into the sauce as it cools—just keep tossing.

Fettuccini with Raw Vegetable Sauce

Pasta from the Kitchen Cupboard

THIS RECIPE REALLY

depends on what's in your kitchen cupboard at any given time. I'm assuming that yours, like mine, will always have a can of anchovies, some dried hot red chili peppers, garlic and the best quality extra-virgin olive oil you can afford — as well as pasta, of course. There might also be a bunch of Italian parsley in the refrigerator or perhaps in an herb garden right outside the kitchen door.

nancy harmon jenkins

SERVES 4 TO 6

6 quarts (5.5 l) water
1 tablespoon salt
1 pound (450 g) spaghetti, linguine, vermicelli, or any other kind of pasta
¼ cup extra-virgin olive oil
4 garlic cloves, minced
4 anchovy fillets, drained and chopped
1 small dried hot red chili pepper, crumbled
About ¼ cup minced fresh Italian parsley
1 tablespoon minced fresh basil, rosemary, savory, or lovage
Sea salt and freshly ground black pepper to taste

METHOD   Have everything ready ahead of time, garlic minced, anchovies chopped, etc., so you can work quickly once you get started.

In a large stockpot, bring the water to a rolling boil. Add the tablespoon of salt, then stir in the pasta to cook for about 10 minutes.

While the pasta is cooking, heat the olive oil in a very large skillet or 6 quart (5.5 l) pot over medium-low heat. Add the garlic and anchovies and cook very gently, crushing the anchovies into the oil with a fork. As soon as the garlic is softened, but not brown, add the crumbled chili and the minced herbs, along with ¼ cup of the pasta cooking water. Turn the heat up and let the sauce simmer.

Meanwhile, when the pasta is cooked to a little firmer than *al dente*, drain it well and immediately turn it into the skillet or pot with the sauce. Mix well, cover and let the pasta simmer in its sauce for about 2 minutes. Taste for salt and pepper then serve immediately.

Pasta with Raw Artichoke Sauce

SERVES 4

2 large or 4 small artichokes
1 lemon, cut in half
6 quarts (5.5 l) water
2 tablespoons sea salt
1 pound (450 g) spaghetti

2 garlic cloves, minced
4 tablespoons extra-virgin olive oil
1 tablespoon minced fresh parsley
Freshly ground black pepper to taste

METHOD   Begin by preparing the artichokes: remove the outer leaves until the base of the leaves is a paler green color. Hold the artichoke in one hand, stem-side-down. Using a serrated knife, carve the artichoke where the leaves are tender, turning it around to create something that looks a bit like a flower bud. Trim the stem and base to remove all tough inedible material. Rub cut surfaces of the artichoke with the lemon half. Slice the artichoke in half lengthwise and remove the fuzzy choke. Slice into wedges as thin as possible, or slice on a mandoline. Squeeze lemon juice over the artichoke slices. Set aside.

In a large stockpot bring the water to a rolling boil. Add the salt and spaghetti and cook until *al dente* (hard), about ¾ done.

While the pasta is cooking, place the minced garlic in a large skillet, drizzle with 2 tablespoons of the olive oil and cook over medium heat until it barely begins to brown. Add the parsley and remove from the heat.

When the pasta has cooked to *al dente*, drain well, reserving 1 cup of the starchy pasta cooking water. Add the drained pasta to the garlic in the skillet. Add ½ cup of the pasta cooking water and cook over the highest heat, stirring with a wooden fork to mix the pasta and garlic. Add more of the pasta cooking water if the sauce dries out or the pasta isn't cooked. Add the remaining 2 tablespoons of olive oil and sprinkle with freshly ground black pepper to taste before serving.

ARTICHOKES MUST BE cleaned with no mercy for this recipe, as the stuff you'd leave on the plate after eating steamed artichokes is the stuff that must be eliminated beforehand, leaving only the tender, edible leaves and heart. As usual, the best extra-virgin yields the best results.

faith willinger

Pasta with Leeks

SERVES 4

5-6 leeks, trimmed and cleaned

4 tablespoons extra-virgin olive oil

1 cup simmering water or homemade
chicken broth

Sea salt and freshly ground black pepper
to taste

6 quarts (5.5 l) water

12-16 ounces (350-450 g) fusilli or
ridged short pasta

1-2 teaspoons minced lemon zest

1 teaspoon minced fresh parsley

Freshly grated Parmigiano Reggiano
cheese, for garnish

METHOD   Split each leek in half and slice into thin half-circles. Place in a 6 quart
(5.5 l) heavy-bottomed stockpot, drizzle with the oil and stir until the leeks are well
coated. Cook over low heat for 10-20 minutes until cooked but not browned. Add the
water or broth, season lightly with salt and freshly ground black pepper and simmer
for 10-20 minutes, until most of the water has evaporated.

In another large pot, bring the 6 quarts (5.5 l) of water to a rolling boil. Add
a pinch of salt and the pasta and cook until quite *al dente* (hard), about ¾ done. Drain
the pasta well, reserving 1 cup of the starchy pasta cooking water.

Add the drained pasta to the sauce in the pot. Add the lemon zest, parsley and
¼ cup of the pasta cooking water and cook over the highest heat, stirring with a
wooden fork to mix the pasta and sauce. Add more starchy water if the sauce dries
out and the pasta isn't cooked. Serve with the Parmigiano Reggiano cheese.

A HINT FROM TORQUATO,
my muse of Tuscan vegetables,
made me substitute leeks for
asparagus in a favorite recipe.
Then, chef Patrizio Cirri
from the winery in Tenuta di
Capezzana, gave the recipe
a new twist.

---

faith willinger

Pasta with Leeks

Pasta with Ricotta and Herb

RICOTTA CHEESE, PLENTY

of fresh herb and black

pepper flavor this speedy

pasta dish.

faith willinger

SERVES 4 TO 6

6 quarts (5.5 l) water
1½ teaspoons sea salt
1 pound (450 g) spaghetti
1 cup whole milk ricotta cheese
2 tablespoons chopped fresh basil,
   Italian parsley, mint, or arugula

¼ teaspoon freshly ground black pepper
½ cup freshly grated pecorino Romano or
   Parmigiano Reggiano cheese

METHOD   In a large stockpot, bring the water to a rolling boil. Add ½ teaspoon of the salt and spaghetti and cook until quite *al dente*, about ¾ done.

   While the pasta is cooking, scoop out ¼ cup of the pasta cooking water. In a food processor or with an immersion mixer, whip the ricotta, the herb, the remaining 1 teaspoon of salt, pepper and ¼ cup pasta cooking water until creamy. Transfer to a very large non-stick skillet or 6 quart (5.5 l) pot.

   When the pasta is cooked to quite *al dente*, drain well, reserving 1 cup of the pasta cooking water. Add the drained pasta to the ricotta cheese in the skillet or pot, along with ¼ cup of the pasta cooking water and ¼ cup of the grated cheese. Cook over the highest heat, stirring with a wooden fork to mix well. Add more of the pasta cooking water if the sauce dries out and the pasta isn't cooked. Serve garnished with the remaining grated cheese.

Capellini Aglio-Olio with Garlic Shrimp

SERVES 4 TO 6

The Aglio-Olio

1 tablespoon minced garlic

½ cup extra-virgin olive oil

1 cup cold water

1 oil-packed anchovy fillet, rinsed and patted dry

Pinch red pepper flakes

The Capellini and Garlic Shrimp

1 tablespoon extra-virgin olive oil

2 cups escarole leaves, cut into ½ inch (1.5 cm) pieces

1 pound (450 g) large shrimp, about 12-16 shrimp, peeled and de-veined

1 tablespoon freshly squeezed lemon juice

1 pound (450 g) capellini pasta, preferably DeCecco

Kosher salt to taste

Freshly grated Parmigiano Reggiano cheese, to pass at the table

METHOD   To cook the capellini, bring a large pot of cold water to a boil.

Meanwhile, make the *aglio-olio*, or garlic-oil. Place the garlic and olive oil in a small sauce-pan set over medium-high heat. Have the water handy. Cook until the garlic begins to brown, about 5 minutes. Add the anchovy fillet and red pepper flakes and cook until the garlic is very brown and fragrant, about 2-3 minutes. Immediately and carefully add the cool water in one smooth stream. Remove from the heat and set aside. The aglio-olio can be made one day in advance. Cover and refrigerate until ready to use.

To finish the capellini and garlic shrimp, set a very large skillet or 6 quart (5.5 l) pot over medium-high heat. When it is hot, add the olive oil and the chopped escarole and cook until the escarole is wilted, about 3 minutes. Add the shrimp and cook until the shrimp begins to turn opaque, about 2 minutes. Add the lemon juice and the aglio-olio and slowly simmer while you cook the capellini pasta.

Add 2 tablespoons of salt and the capellini to the boiling water and cook until the pasta is flexible enough to fit into the skillet or pot, about 1½ minutes. Scoop out 2 cups of the pasta cooking water and set aside. Drain the pasta well, then add immediately to the simmering skillet or pot. Cook until the pasta is tender and has absorbed the liquid. If the pan dries out before the pasta is tender, add some of the reserved pasta cooking water. Taste for salt and serve, passing the cheese at the table.

HINT   I boil the pasta only until it is flexible enough to fit in my skillet with the shrimp and sauce; that way the pasta will absorb the liquid in the pan along with its flavor.

ANGEL HAIR PASTA—*capelli di angelo* in Italian—is so popular in the United States. In this recipe I love pairing the capellini with the smoky flavor of garlic that is cooked in olive oil to a deep, deep brown. Please do not be scared off by the anchovy in this recipe—I guarantee that no one will be able to tell that it is there and the anchovy does add a nice round dimension to this dish. When you purchase your shrimp please be sure to select shrimp that are sweet smelling and nicely translucent.

joe simone

Tagliatelle with Asparagus and Cream

I LEARNED HOW TO

prepare this pasta from

Giovanna of Trattoria

Pandemonio in Florence.

Giovanna comes to work

each morning and prepares

the pasta and other time

consuming items and then

is the captain of her dining

room when the restaurant

is open. Her son Francesco

mans the stoves during

service. The secret of this

pasta is to thoroughly

imbue the sauce with the

rich flavor of asparagus.

The result is divine — and

the asparagus will NOT be

vibrant green and crunchy.

The asparagus will be very

tender — almost melting.

joe simone

SERVES 2 TO 4

1 bunch fresh asparagus, ends trimmed
  and discarded
Pinch kosher or sea salt to taste
1 teaspoon unsalted butter
½ cup chicken stock

½ cup heavy whipping cream
½ pound (225 g) fresh tagliatelle pasta
  or good quality dried fettuccini
1 tablespoon freshly grated Parmigiano
  Reggiano cheese or to taste

METHOD Bring a large pot of cold water to the boil. Meanwhile, cut the asparagus into small pieces. When the water boils, add a generous pinch of salt and cook the asparagus for 1 minute. Drain, reserving the water for cooking the pasta.

Add the asparagus to a large skillet along with the butter, cook over medium-high heat until the butter sizzles and the asparagus becomes fragrant. Add the chicken stock and simmer until the stock is reduced almost to a paste, about 4 minutes. Add the cream and simmer until thickened.

Bring the pot filled with the reserved asparagus cooking water to the boil. Cook the tagliatelle pasta for 1-2 minutes (about double that time if using dried pasta). Scoop out 1 cup of the pasta cooking water and reserve. Drain the pasta well.

Add the pasta to the simmering cream mixture and cook until the sauce has thickened around the pasta. Immediately add the Parmigiano Reggiano cheese and toss until well combined. If the sauce seems a bit dry, add a little of the reserved pasta cooking water.

Taste for salt and serve immediately, passing the pepper mill and freshly grated Parmigiano Reggiano cheese.

INGREDIENTS TIP If you cannot find excellent thin, fresh pasta you should use dried fettuccine or even egg noodles. Do not use commercial prepared fresh pasta found in your deli case as it is too thick and seems to always cook up mealy for me.

Tagliatelle with Asparagus and Cream

Pasta with Tuna Fish and Caper Sauce

SERVES 4

6 quarts (5.5 l) water
2 tablespoons sea salt
1 pound (450 g) spaghetti or linguine pasta
2 garlic cloves, minced
3 tablespoons extra-virgin olive oil
⅛ teaspoon dried red pepper flakes
1 teaspoon chopped fresh parsley

½-¾ pound (225-350 g) tomatoes, seeded, juiced and chopped or 1 cup of canned diced tomato or drained plum tomatoes
2 tablespoons capers, packed in salt, rinsed
8-10 ounces (225-300 g) tuna, packed in oil, drained and crumbled, or leftover cooked tuna

METHOD   In a large stockpot, bring the water to a rolling boil. Add the salt and spaghetti and cook until quite _al dente_ (hard), about ¾ done.

While the pasta is cooking, place the garlic in a large skillet, drizzle with the oil and cook over low heat until the garlic just begins to color. Add the chili pepper, parsley, tomatoes and capers and simmer over medium-high heat for 2-3 minutes. Add the crumbled tuna, stir and lower the heat to keep the sauce warm.

When the pasta is cooked to quite _al dente_, drain well, reserving 1 cup of the starchy pasta cooking water. Add the drained pasta to the sauce in the skillet. Pour in ¼ cup of the pasta cooking water and cook over the highest heat, stirring with a wooden fork to mix the pasta and sauce. Add more of the pasta cooking water if the sauce dries out and the pasta isn't cooked. Serve immediately.

HINT   If the capers look at all dried out, soak them for 10 minutes.

Pasta with Tuna Fish and Caper Sauce

Wild Mushroom Ravioli in Asparagus Cream

SERVES 4 TO 6

The Wild Mushroom Ravioli

1 pound (450 g) wild mushrooms, preferably morel

6 tablespoons unsalted butter

Pinch red pepper flakes or to taste

½ cup dry red wine

1 tablespoon heavy whipping cream

¼ cup freshly grated whole milk mozzarella cheese

2 tablespoons, plus additional to garnish, freshly grated Pamigiano Reggiano cheese

Kosher or sea salt to taste

1 package won ton wrappers

1 egg mixed with 1 tablespoon water

The Asparagus Cream

1 pound (450 g) asparagus, ends trimmed and discarded

1 tablespoon unsalted butter

½ cup diced onion

1 cup chicken or vegetable stock

1 cup heavy whipping cream

METHOD   For the wild mushroom ravioli, thoroughly clean the mushrooms. Cut off stems where appropriate and cut the mushrooms into ½ inch (1.5 cm) pieces.

In a large skillet melt the butter. When bubbling add the red pepper flakes and cook 1 minute. Add the mushrooms and cook over medium heat until the mushrooms give off their moisture, about 5 minutes. Add the red wine, a generous pinch of kosher or sea salt and the cream, raise the heat and cook until the wine is absorbed and the mushrooms are quite tender.

Transfer the contents of the skillet to a food processor or blender with a steel blade and pulse several times until the mushrooms are finely cut, but not a paste. Transfer to a mixing bowl and let cool for 15 minutes.

To the cooled vegetables, add the grated mozzarella, 2 tablespoons of Parmigiano Reggiano cheese and stir well. Taste for salt. Cover with plastic wrap and refrigerate for at least 1 hour or overnight.

To fill the ravioli, place 24 of the won ton wrappers on a work surface. Divide the filling among the wrappers and brush the edges of the wrappers with the egg and water mixture. Carefully place another won ton wrapper over each "filled" skin and crimp down to create a seal. I use a pastry wheel to cut the won ton wrappers, thereby creating a seal. Place on a clean and dry baking sheet and freeze for 4 hours. Remove from the freezer and transfer carefully to zip-lock plastic bags. They will store for weeks in your freezer.

PLEASE DO NOT BE SCARED off by this recipe's perceived complexity! Instead, think of it in stages. On the first day, you can prepare the mushroom filling and refrigerate it. On the second day, fill the ravioli (you can enlist some helpers—kids love to do this). Then freeze the ravioli on cookie sheets lubricated with pan release.

The next day, transfer the ravioli to zip-lock bags and store them in your freezer until you want to serve the ravioli. The asparagus cream can be prepared one day in advance and refrigerated. So on the day you serve this dish all you have to do is boil the ravioli and toss them in the reheated asparagus cream. Not bad, huh?

joe simone

For the asparagus cream, in a large stockpot filled with boiling water, blanch the asparagus until just beginning to get tender, about 2 minutes. Drain well and refresh under cold running water. Cut into ½ inch (1.5 cm) pieces, reserving the tips separately for garnish.

Melt the butter in a medium saucepan set on medium heat. Add the onion and cook until it wilts, about 5 minutes. Add the chopped asparagus steams and cook until the asparagus is fragrant, about 2 minutes. Pour in the chicken stock, bring to a brisk simmer and cook until the stock has reduced by two thirds, about 5 minutes. Add the cream and simmer until a nice sauce consistency is reached and the asparagus is very tender. Purée the mixture in a blender, food processor or use an immersion blender. Taste for salt. This sauce can be used immediately or cooled down and stored overnight, covered, in the refrigerator.

To serve, bring a large pot of water to a boil. Add a pinch of salt and cook the ravioli. In a large skillet, warm the sauce very gently. When the ravioli is done, drain well then transfer to the skillet with the sauce. Toss gently until well coated. Warm the asparagus tips in a little melted butter. Serve in individual bowls, garnished with the asparagus tips. Pass the pepper mill and some of the Parmigiano Reggiano cheese.

INGREDIENTS TIP   I think that using won ton wrappers, while being unconventional in the Italian kitchen, will save you a lot of time and does produce excellent results. Won ton wrappers are available at most supermarkets in the refrigerated food or produce section.

Orrechiette with Garlic Sausage and Rapini

ORRECHIETTE ARE PASTA

formed in the shape of "little

ears." From the region of

Apulia, the heel of the Italian

boot this small pasta used to

be only formed by a process

of dragging a small nugget

of pasta dough across your

thumb. A few years back I

had the opportunity to make

orrechiette with three

generations of Italian women

in the Apulian city of Lecce.

I cannot say that I mastered

the art of orrechiette form-

ing—the women said my

thumbs were too thick!

joe simone

SERVES 4 TO 6

2 bunches rapini (broccoli rabe), trimmed
Kosher or sea salt to taste
½ pound (225 g) bulk garlic or Italian
    sausage
¼ cup extra-virgin olive oil
Pinch red pepper flakes or to taste

2 tablespoons chopped fresh parsley
1 pound (450 g) orrechiette pasta
½ cup dried breadcrumbs
Freshly grated Parmigiano Reggiano or
    Romano cheese, for garnish

METHOD   Bring a large pot of cold water to the boil. Add the salt and cook the rapini until just beginning to be tender, about 2-3 minutes. Drain immediately then rinse under cold running water. Chop into bite-size pieces. This can be done up to 12 hours in advance. Simply cover the rapini and refrigerate until ready to use.

Rinse out the pot, fill with cold water and bring to a boil.

Meanwhile, brown the sausage in a large skillet set on medium-high heat. Pour off half of the sausage fat and return the pan to the heat. Add the olive oil and cook for 2 minutes. Add the red pepper flakes and parsley and cook for 2 minutes. Add the rapini, turn the heat to low and barely simmer while you cook the pasta.

Add a generous pinch of salt to the boiling water and cook the orrechiette until barely tender. Scoop out 2 cups of the pasta cooking water and set aside. Drain the pasta well and add to the simmering sausage mixture. Add enough of the reserved water to make a sauce, raise the heat and cook until the pasta is just *al dente* and the sauce has thickened, adding more water if needed. Toss in the breadcrumbs to help the sauce adhere to the pasta. Taste for salt. Serve immediately with plenty of grated Parmigiano or Romano cheese.

INGREDIENTS TIPS   Rapini is also known as rabe or broccoli rabe and is a wonderfully bitter cousin of our broccoli. Do not let its bitter flavor dissuade you from making this recipe.

If your meat market sells sausage out of the casing—great! If not simply remove the casings before preparing this recipe.

Also, a note on the breadcrumbs: I use day old bread with the crust removed and then whirl it in my food processor until finely ground.

Orrechiette with Garlic Sausage and Rapini

Farfalle Pasta with Spicy Portobello Mushrooms and Tomato

THIS IS A "TAKE OFF"

on the classic Italian sauce arrabiata. *Arrabiata* means "angry" in Italian, and this sauce is always a combination of ground tomatoes, chile peppers and other seasonings. I like the non-traditional pairing of portobello mushrooms with the tomato paste, spice and cognac. This sauce is simple to prepare and is silken and delicious.

joe simone

SERVES 6 TO 8

1 tablespoon extra-virgin olive oil
1 tablespoon unsalted butter
2 teaspoons minced garlic
Pinch red pepper flakes
1½ pounds (750 g) portobello mushrooms,
   stems removed and cut into thin strips
¼ cup chopped fresh parsley
⅛ cup cognac or brandy

1 tablespoon tomato paste
1 cup water
1 pound (450 g) farfalle pasta
Kosher or sea salt and black pepper
   to taste
Freshly grated Parmigiano Reggiano
   cheese, for garnish

METHOD   Bring a large pot of cold water to the boil to cook the farfalle pasta.
     Meanwhile, heat the olive oil and butter in a very large skillet or 6 quart (5.5 l) pot. When hot, add the garlic and sauté until fragrant. Add the red pepper flakes peppers and portobello mushrooms and cook for 3 minutes. Add the chopped parsley and cook for 1 minute. Carefully deglaze with the cognac or brandy. Add the tomato paste and water and reduce by one third. Keep at a low simmer.
     When the large pot of water is boiling, cook the farfalle pasta according to the directions on the box. Scoop out 1 cup of the pasta cooking water and set aside. When done, drain the pasta then transfer to the skillet or pot with the sauce. Toss the pasta, adding some of the reserved pasta cooking water if the pan is too dry. Taste for salt and pepper. Serve in warm bowls, passing the cheese and pepper mill at the table.

HINT   I always reserve some of the pasta cooking water to adjust the texture of my finished sauce. This water has some of the starch from the pasta in it and will help bind the sauce to the noodles.

Ricotta Gnocchi with Wild Mushrooms and Sage Butter

SERVES 4 TO 6

The Ricotta Gnocchi

1 cup ricotta cheese, drained

½ cup unbleached all-purpose flour

4 egg yolks

1 tablespoon chopped fresh parsley

1¼ cups freshly grated Parmigiano
    Reggiano cheese

The Sage Butter

1 pound (450 g) unsalted butter

1 bunch fresh sage, about ½ ounce (15 g)

For Serving

¼ cup extra-virgin olive oil

1 pound (450 g) wild mushrooms, stems
    removed and discarded

1 teaspoon kosher or sea salt or to taste

Freshly grated Parmigiano Reggiano
    cheese, for garnish

I HATE THE TOUGH, LEADEN gnocchi usually found in the United States! These gnocchi are light as a feather and utterly delicious with the mushroom and sage butter sauce. Please do not skimp on the quality of the Parmigiano you use and grate it as fine as possible.

joe simone

METHOD   For the ricotta gnocchi, put the ricotta cheese in a medium stainless steel mixing bowl and stir gently with a fork to break up any lumps. Add the flour and mix well with the fork. Add the egg yolks and stir with the fork until combined. Add the parsley and cheese and stir with the fork until the dough begins to come together. Transfer the dough to a lightly floured board and knead gently until the dough is smooth and homogenous. Don't be tempted to add too much flour to the board. The dough may be a little sticky but that's okay. Cover and refrigerate for at least 30 minutes. The dough can be held covered in the refrigerator overnight.

Using 2 soup spoons, form small oval balls (quenelles) about ¼ ounce (7 g) each. Place on a lightly floured baking sheet, cover and refrigerate until ready to serve.

For the sage butter, slowly melt the butter in a small saucepan. Raise the heat and skim off the foam as it forms. Remove the sage leaves off the stems and discard the stems. When all the foam is skimmed, add the sage leaves and cook for 2 minutes. Immediately remove from the heat and let cool.

To serve, add the olive oil to a very hot skillet. Add the mushrooms, season with the salt and cook until the mushrooms are seared, about 4 minutes. Meanwhile, in a large pot of boiling water, add a pinch of salt and cook the gnocchi until they float to the surface, about 2 minutes. Add the sage butter to the cooked mushrooms and taste for salt. Drain the gnocchi very well and add to the mushrooms. Toss very gently just to coat with the sauce. Serve on individual plates or a large warmed patter. Pass the Parmigiano Reggiano cheese on the side.

HINTS   These gnocchi can be frozen for up to two weeks. Simply take them from your freezer and drop them in boiling water.

The action of forming the gnocchi with two spoons may seem difficult at first but do not lose heart! You will soon become comfortable with the spoons and once you try these gnocchi you will want to make this recipe often.

Andalucian Gazpacho

doing in an Italian kitchen?
Think of it as a variation of
the Tuscan bread-and-tomato
salad called *panzanella*. When
tomatoes arrived in the
Mediterranean around 1492,
gazpacho was a humble and,
frankly, not terribly interesting peasant soup made of stale
bread, olive oil and vinegar.
It took the brilliant red fruit
from America to carry gazpacho to gastronomic heights.
Try this on a hot summer
day at the peak of the tomato
season.

nancy harmon jenkins

SERVES 6

3½ pounds (1.6 kg) ripe red tomatoes, peeled, seeded and chopped

2 garlic cloves, chopped

1 small red onion, chopped

½ cup extra-virgin olive oil, preferably Andalucian

2 tablespoons aged sherry wine vinegar or more to taste

1 (2 inch) (5 cm) slice stale country-style bread, crusts removed

½ cup cold water

½ teaspoon ground cumin

Pinch of cayenne pepper

Sea salt and sugar to taste

Garnishes: Finely diced cucumber, green bell pepper or red onion; tiny toasted croutons, and/or chopped hard-boiled egg

METHOD Mix together the tomatoes, garlic and onion, and working in batches, whirl the mixture briefly in a blender or food processor, just enough to make a rather chunky purée. Remove each batch to another bowl as it's done. With the last batch, add the olive oil and vinegar as you process, pouring the oil slowly as you would with a mayonnaise so that it emulsifies. Do not remove the last batch from the blender or processor yet.

Tear the bread into smaller pieces and soak briefly in the cold water. Gently squeeze out the excess water and add the softened bread to the last batch, along with the cumin and cayenne. Whirl to incorporate thoroughly. Now stir the contents of the blender or processor into the rest of the vegetables, mixing thoroughly.

Taste for salt or sugar if necessary — ¼ teaspoon of sugar will bring out the flavor of the tomatoes. More vinegar may also be added. If the soup is too thick, stir in ice-cold water until the consistency is right. If it's too thin, a little more bread or puréed vegetables will thicken it. The right consistency is a matter of personal taste.

In order to appreciate the full tomato flavor, gazpacho should be served chilled but not icy cold. Garnish with any or all of the traditional garnishes listed above.

Andalucian Gazpacho

Angelo's Hearty Two Step Minestrone

I LEARNED TO MAKE THIS

soup years ago from Angelo

Pellegrini, an immigrant lad

who went on to become a

much-loved English professor

at the University of Wash-

ington and one of Seattle's

most respected food gurus. It's

abundant enough to be a one

dish (or one bowl) meal. It's

called "two step" because you

can make the bean soup one

day, then use the leftovers to

finish the dish.

nancy harmon jenkins

SERVES 4 TO 6

1 cup dried cannellini or borlotti beans,
    soaked overnight
4 sprigs fresh thyme
3 cups water
6 cups chicken stock, preferably homemade
2 tablespoons extra-virgin olive oil
1 tablespoon finely minced pancetta
    or prosciutto
1 large onion, chopped
3 garlic cloves, minced
3 stalks celery, thinly sliced
¼ cup minced fresh flat-leaf parsley

2 large tomatoes, peeled and chopped, or
    1 cup canned whole tomatoes, chopped
    with their juice
1 carrot, peeled and diced
1 large potato, peeled and diced
½ small Savoy cabbage, slivered
5 or 6 leaves green or red chard, slivered
5 or 6 leaves Lacinto (Tuscan) kale,
    if available
1 zucchini, diced
½ cup slivered fresh basil leaves
1½-2 cups cooked elbow pasta or cooked
    rice, if desired
Salt and freshly ground black pepper to taste

METHOD   Drain the beans and transfer to a large saucepan. Add 2 sprigs of the thyme, 1 cup of the water and 1 cup of the stock and bring to a simmer over medium-low heat. Cover and cook gently until the beans are tender, about 40 minutes to 1 hour, depending on the age of the dried beans. Pour the remaining water and stock into separate small saucepans and bring to a simmer. Check the beans while cooking, adding alternating cups of stock and water as the beans absorb the liquid in the pan. You will probably need about 2 cups stock and 2 cups water during the cooking process. Reserve at least 3 cups of stock to use later. When the beans are tender, remove them from the heat. Pick out the thyme sprigs and discard. In a food processor or blender, purée the beans with their liquid, cover and set aside.

Pour the olive oil into a heavy stockpot over medium-low heat and gently sauté the pancetta or prosciutto until it is melted but not brown, about 5 minutes. Add the onion, garlic, celery, parsley and remaining thyme and cook, stirring occasionally, until the vegetables start to soften, about 10 minutes. Add the tomatoes and 1 cup of the remaining stock, cover and cook over medium-low heat for about 10 minutes.

Add the carrot and potato to the pot and cook until the vegetables start to soften, about 10 minutes. Stir in the cabbage, chard, kale and zucchini and mix well. Cover and cook for 10 minutes. Add the bean purée and the remaining stock to make a thick but still liquid soup. Taste, adding salt and pepper if desired. Cover and cook over low heat for 15-20 minutes, or until the greens are tender.

When the soup is ready to serve, remove it from the heat and stir in the basil and cooked pasta or rice, if desired. Minestrone may be served hot, with freshly grated Parmigiano cheese sprinkled over the top. During the hot summer months in northern Italy minestrone is often served at room temperature. It is called *Minestrone Fredda*, although it is not really *fredda* or cold. If serving at room temperature, omit the cheese.

HINT   To make a vegetarian minestrone, use all water instead of chicken stock, and omit the pancetta, increasing the olive oil to 2 tablespoons.

Bean Soup with Shrimp alla Titanic

SERVES 4

3 cups cooked beans

1½ cups bean cooking water or light vegetable stock

1 tablespoon extra-virgin olive oil, plus 4 tablespoons extra-virgin olive oil, for garnish

1 garlic clove, chopped

½ teaspoon sea salt

1 teaspoon minced fresh parsley

4 slices rustic country-style bread, lightly toasted

¾ pound (350 g) cooked shelled shrimp

¼ teaspoon freshly ground black pepper

BEANS ARE PAIRED WITH shrimp in this classic, easy-to-prepare Tuscan appetizer. It is named "Titanic" for its sea of bean broth, in which floats a raft of toast and a few shrimp, some on, some off the raft.

faith willinger

METHOD   In a blender or food processor, purée 1 cup of the cooked beans with the cooking water or broth. Drizzle 2 tablespoons of the olive oil into a 2 quart (2 l) stockpot over medium-low heat and sauté the garlic until it barely begins to color, about 2 minutes. Add the bean purée broth, the remaining beans, salt and pepper to taste, bring to a simmer and cook, uncovered, for 10-15 minutes. Stir in the chopped parsley.

To serve, ladle the bean soup into bowls. Float a "raft" of toast in each bowl. Top each "raft" with a few of the shrimp and drizzle each serving with 1 tablespoon of the extra-virgin olive oil. Garnish with more of the pepper, if desired.

"Cooked Water" Vegetable Soup
Acquacotta

ALTHOUGH ITS NAME

means "cooked water," this

Tuscan soup is full of flavor.

Topped with a poached

egg and grated cheese, this

first course could easily

become a whole meal.

faith willinger

SERVES 4

1 large red onion, roughly chopped

4-6 stalks celery, roughly chopped

3-4 tablespoons extra-virgin olive oil

1 cup tomato pulp (seeded, juiced and
  chopped fresh tomatoes, canned diced
  tomatoes or drained and chopped
  canned plum tomatoes)

Pinch of dried red pepper flakes (optional)

4 cups water or homemade chicken or
  vegetable broth, simmering

½ teaspoon sea salt

2 teaspoons chopped fresh parsley

4 slices rustic country-style bread,
  lightly toasted

4 eggs

¼ cup freshly grated Parmigiano Reggiano,
  for garnish

METHOD   In a 3 quart (2.75 l) heavy-bottomed non-reactive stockpot mix the onion and celery with the oil and stir until well coated. Place the pot over medium-low heat and cook until the onion is cooked but not brown, about 10-12 minutes. Add the tomatoes, chili pepper and simmering water or broth, season lightly to taste with the salt and cook, uncovered, over low heat for 20-30 minutes. The vegetables should be very soft. Stir in the parsley.

To serve, place 1 slice of the toasted bread in individual soup bowls. Poach the eggs in the broth. Remove with a slotted spoon and top each slice of bread with an egg. Ladle the soup and vegetables over each egg and garnish with a sprinkle of the Parmigiano Reggiano cheese.

"Cooked Water" Vegetable Soup
(Acquacotta)

Butternut Squash Soup with Amaretti and Crispy Prosciutto

SERVES 6 GENEROUSLY

2 pounds (900 g) butternut squash, peeled and cut into ½ inch (1.5 cm) cubes

¼ cup plus 2 tablespoons extra-virgin olive oil

2 tablespoons unsalted butter

4 ounces (115 g) prosciutto, thinly sliced

2 cinnamon sticks

½ pound (225 g) sweet onion, preferably Spanish, cut into ½ inch (1.5 cm) dice

½ pound (225 g) carrots, peeled and cut into ½ inch (1.5 cm) dice

½ pound (225 g) celery, cut into ½ inch (1.5 cm) dice

1 heaping tablespoon fresh chopped sage leaves

2 quarts (2 l) chicken stock

18 amaretti cookies or to taste

½ cup heavy whipping cream

Kosher or sea salt and freshly ground black pepper to taste

METHOD   Preheat the oven to 400°F (200°C). In a large bowl toss the butternut squash with 2 tablespoons of the olive oil, butter, and salt to taste. Transfer to a large baking sheet in a single layer and roast until caramelized and tender, about 20 minutes, stirring occasionally.

While the squash is roasting, heat the remaining ¼ cup of olive oil in a tall stockpot over medium heat. Add the prosciutto and cook, stirring often, until the prosciutto gets very crispy and deep red. Transfer with a slotted spoon, being careful for splattering oil, to paper towels until ready to serve.

To the same pot, immediately add the cinnamon sticks, onion, carrots and celery and cook over medium heat for 10 minutes. Remove the pot from the heat and set aside until the squash is finished cooking.

When the squash is done, remove from the oven and transfer the squash to the stockpot with the cooked vegetables. Add the sage and cook over medium-high heat, stirring, for 1 minute. Add the chicken stock, bring to a simmer, and cook for 10 minutes. Crumble 15 of the amaretti cookies into the stockpot and cook for 5 minutes, until the soup begins to thicken and the crumbled cookies become engorged.

Remove the cinnamon sticks and purée in a food processor or blender in batches. Return the soup to the pot, add the cream, bring back to a gentle simmer and taste for salt and pepper.

To serve, ladle into individual bowls and top with the crispy prosciutto and the remaining amaretti cookies, coarsely crumbled.

HINT   You may have to adjust the amount of stock needed. Be sure to barely cover the ingredients in the stock pot.

Butternut Squash Soup with Amaretti and Crispy Prosciutto

THIS IS A CREAMY SOUP that uses very little cream. The richness comes from slowly roasting the squash and then cooking "close" to the stock. In other words you use just enough stock to cover the squash, with the top of the stock staying "close" to the other ingredients in the soup. The amaretti cookies provide some thickening as well as a wonderful sweet complement to the soup, and cinnamon sticks are one of my favorite seasonings.

joe simone

Chicken and Escarole Soup with Pasta and Pork and Sage Meatballs

SERVES 6 TO 8

The Pork and Sage Meatballs

1 pound (450 g) ground pork

½ cup loosely packed, chopped fresh sage leaves

½ cup freshly grated Parmigiano Reggiano cheese

1 cup dried breadcrumbs

¼ teaspoon kosher or sea salt or to taste

2 eggs, lightly beaten

¼ cup milk or as needed

The Chicken and Escarole Soup

1 (3½ pound) (1.6 kg) chicken, cut into 8 pieces

2 quarts (2 l) chicken stock

2 tablespoons extra-virgin olive oil

2 tablespoons unsalted butter

1 cup diced sweet onion, preferably Spanish

1 cup diced carrot

1 cup diced celery

3 cups packed diced escarole

Kosher or sea salt and freshly ground black pepper to taste

1½ cups tiny pasta, preferably acini di pepe or pastina

Freshly grated Parmigiano Reggiano cheese, for garnish

METHOD   For the meatballs, in a large bowl add the pork, sage, cheese and breadcrumbs and mix well. Season with the salt. Add the beaten eggs and mix well. Add milk as needed to create a tight, but not wet, texture. In a small skillet, quickly fry a small piece of the meat mixture and taste for salt. Correct the seasoning as needed.

Preheat the oven to 375°F (190°C). Lightly oil a baking sheet. Shape the meat into tiny (½ inch) (1.5 cm) meatballs and place them on the prepared baking sheet. Roast for 5 minutes in the preheated oven or until cooked through. Remove from the oven and set aside.

For the soup, rinse the chicken well and transfer to a large stockpot. Pour in the chicken stock, bring to a simmer and cook for 20 minutes, skimming the fat as needed, until the chicken is cooked through. Transfer the chicken pieces to a platter and set aside until cool enough to handle. Set the chicken stock aside.

Remove the chicken skin and discard. Pick the chicken off the bones and discard the bones. Set aside the picked over chicken meat.

Heat the olive oil and butter in a large stockpot over medium-high heat. When the butter has melted, add the carrots, onion and celery and cook for 10 minutes, stirring often, until the vegetables are tender and beginning to carmelize. Add the escarole, season generously with salt to taste and cook until the escarole wilts, about 3 minutes. Add the reserved chicken broth and bring to a simmer. Cook for 5 minutes to set the flavor. Add the pasta and simmer for 5 minutes or until the pasta is cooked. Add the cooked chicken and meatballs and simmer for 3 minutes. Serve immediately, passing the pepper mill and grated cheese.

HINT   The trick here is to cook the vegetables until they get really sweet and soft before adding the escarole. Yumm!

Fabio's Farinata, Cornmeal and Kale Soup

SERVES 4

½ pound (225 g) kale or cabbage
6 cups water
1½ teaspoons sea salt
¾ cup cornmeal
4 garlic cloves, minced

¼ cup extra-virgin olive oil, plus 4 tablespoons, for garnish
½ cup freshly grated Parmigiano Reggiano
  cheese
Freshly ground black pepper to taste

METHOD   Wash the kale or cabbage. Remove the tough central ribs of the kale or the core of the cabbage. Chop the leaves finely. In a 3 quart (2.75 l) pot bring the water to a rolling boil. Add the salt and kale or cabbage and cook, simmering, for 5 minutes. Gradually sprinkle in the cornmeal, stirring with a whisk to prevent lumps. Cook over the lowest heat, stirring occasionally, for 20-25 minutes or until creamy. Alternatively, you could place a pot in a larger pot of boiling water—an improvised double boiler—and cook for 45 minutes.

Add the garlic and cook for 5 minutes. Whisk in the grated cheese and ¼ cup of the extra-virgin olive oil and serve immediately. Ladle into bowls and drizzle each portion with 1 tablespoon of the extra-virgin olive oil and freshly grated pepper to taste.

I LEARNED THIS VERSION of farinata from Fabio Picchi, owner-chef of Cibreo, my favorite restaurant in Florence. Cabbage can be substituted for kale if it's not available.

faith willinger

CHAPTER
THREE

Main Courses

IN ITALIAN CUISINE, the dishes considered *secondo piatto*, what we call the main course can greatly vary in quantity and richness, depending on the first course of the meal. In restaurants, it is usual not to order the entire dinner at once. As a waiter in Rome once explained to me, "How do you know now what you're going to want to eat after the pasta?"

At home, we can be better menu planners. It is wise to serve a lighter second after a hearty pasta. A lighter pasta dish or a soup or salad might call for something a bit more substantial to follow. For holidays, special occasions or grand feasts, one might choose to go all out. As all things gastronomic, in Italy these menu decisions are determined by the seasons and the expected appetites of the guests.

Spring Lamb with Garden Vegetables

LAMB IS A SPRINGTIME dish all over the Mediterranean and especially loved for Easter feasting. The oregano and lemon juice in this treatment mean the recipe comes from southern Italy or Greece, but you'll find similar combinations of lamb with young new garden vegetables everywhere from Spain to Turkey and back again.

nancy harmon jenkins

SERVES 6 TO 8

1 (3-4 pound) (1.4-1.8 kg) boneless leg or shoulder of lamb, tied in butcher's twine
2-3 garlic cloves, sliced
1 tablespoon dried oregano
3 tablespoons extra-virgin olive oil
3 tablespoons freshly squeezed lemon juice
1 lemon for preparing the artichokes
8 artichokes
16 small new potatoes, peeled
2 tablespoons tomato paste stirred into ¼ cup water
16 small carrots (about 2 inches (5 cm) long), scraped
16 small white onions, peeled
2 cups shelled young peas
Finely chopped fresh Italian parsley, for garnish
Sea salt and freshly ground black pepper to taste

METHOD Preheat the oven to 450°F (230°C). Using a sharp knife, make little slits about ½ inch (1.5 cm) deep in the surface of the lamb and insert the slivers of garlic. Season the lamb liberally with the salt, pepper and half the oregano, rubbing the seasoning into the lamb with the olive oil. Set the lamb on a rack in a roasting pan, pour the lemon juice over the top, and cook in the preheated oven for 30 minutes.

While the lamb is cooking, prepare the artichokes. Squeeze half of the lemon into a bowl of cool water. Remove the tough outer leaves of the artichokes to expose the tender heart. Cut the artichokes into quarters and scrape out the chokes. As you work, rub the cut surfaces of the artichokes with the remaining lemon half to keep them from browning. Toss the finished artichokes into the cold lemon water until ready to cook.

In a medium bowl, combine the potatoes with the tomato paste mixed with water and a sprinkle of the salt and mix well.

Remove the lamb from the oven and reduce the heat to 350°F (180°C). Add the potatoes and carrots to the roasting pan, sprinkling with the remaining oregano. Roast for 30 minutes. Remove from the oven. Drain the artichokes and add to the roasting pan, along with the onions and 1 cup of water. Return to the oven to cook until the lamb is done to taste. In Greece and southern Italy, lamb is considered best when it's very well done. This will take another 90 minutes. For slightly pink lamb, roast in the oven an additional 60 minutes only. Baste the meat and vegetables every 15 minutes or so with the pan juices.

While the lamb is roasting, bring a pot of water to a rolling boil. Drop in the shelled peas and boil for 5 minutes. Drain well and refresh under cold running water. Add the peas to the roasting pan for the last 20 minutes of cooking.

Serve the lamb on a large platter, surrounded by the vegetables and garnished with the parsley.

Spring Lamb with Garden Vegetables

Grilled Chicken Paillard with Spinach and Golden Raisins

SERVES 4

¼ cup golden raisins
4 (4 ounce) (115 g) boneless, skinless chicken breasts
3 tablespoons extra-virgin olive oil
Kosher or sea salt to taste

2 teaspoons minced garlic
4 cups loosely packed spinach leaves, cleaned and stemmed
1 tablespoon freshly squeezed lemon juice
Lemon wedges, for garnish

METHOD   Put the raisins in a heatproof container, cover with ½ cup boiling water and set aside.

Light a grill or preheat a broiler. Lay a large piece of plastic wrap on a work surface. Place the chicken breasts on top in a single layer. Cover with another piece of plastic wrap and gently pound the chicken breasts until they are uniformly ¼ inch (6 mm) thick. Remove and discard the top plastic wrap layer and brush the chicken with 1 tablespoon of the olive oil and sprinkle with salt.

When the grill or broiler is hot, grill or broil the breasts until the chicken is just cooked through, about 2 minutes per side. Remove the chicken from the heat and set aside, covered with aluminum foil to keep warm.

Heat a large skillet over medium-high heat. When hot, add the remaining 2 tablespoons of the olive oil and the garlic. Cook until the garlic becomes fragrant, about 2 minutes. Add the spinach and stir until the spinach wilts, about 3 minutes. Drain the plumped raisins and add to the pan. Pour in the lemon juice and season with salt to taste.

To serve, place a chicken breast on each plate and top with some of the spinach. Pass the pepper mill and some additional lemon wedges.

INGREDIENTS TIP   I like to use the California leaf variety of spinach. It comes in a bunch like lettuce versus the cello wrapped spinach that always smells odd to me and requires much cleaning.

SPINACH COOKED WITH garlic and raisins is popular all over Italy. In this recipe, they are served with chicken paillards. Now a paillard is simply something pounded very thin. Quickly cooking a boneless and skinless breast of chicken that has been pounded to a uniform ¼ inch (6 mm) thickness is not only very easy to prepare but will also produce a delicious, tender meal. However, be sure not to overcook the chicken or it will be very tough and dry! I would also suggest serving this dish with new potatoes, quartered and roasted with olive oil and salt.

joe simone

Lemon Braised Chicken with Polenta

SERVES 4 TO 6

The Lemon Chicken

1 (3½ pound) (1.6 kg) chicken, cut into
   8 pieces

¼ cup extra-virgin olive oil

8 garlic cloves, smashed

18 fresh sage leaves, whole with no stem

½ cup chopped carrots, cut into ¼ inch
   (6 mm) dice

½ cup chopped celery, cut into ¼ inch
   (6 mm) dice

½ cup chopped onion, cut into ¼ inch
   (6 mm) dice

½ cup chopped fennel, cut into ¼ inch
   (6 mm) dice

½ cup chopped red bell pepper, cut into
   ¼ inch (6 mm) dice

¼ cup freshly squeezed lemon juice

1 cup chicken stock

Kosher or sea salt to taste

The Polenta

4 cups cold water

1 tablespoon extra-virgin olive oil

1 teaspoon salt

1 cup coarse cornmeal, preferably Gray's
   organic stoneground coarse or Goya

¼ cup chopped fresh chives or parsley

2 tablespoons unsalted butter

½ cup freshly grated Parmigiano
   Reggiano cheese

METHOD   For the chicken, wash the chicken well, pat it dry and season all sides with salt. Heat a large skillet or rondo, large enough to hold the chicken in one layer, over medium-high heat. Add the olive oil and the chicken pieces, skin-side-down. Cook, undisturbed, until the chicken is beginning to brown, about 4 minutes. Add the garlic and sage around the chicken pieces and cook until the chicken skin is well browned, about 2 minutes longer. Turn the chicken pieces over, add the diced vegetables, lemon juice and stock and bring to a simmer. Turn the heat down to low and simmer slowly, covered, until the chicken is very tender, about 30 minutes. Taste the juices for salt.

   While the chicken is cooking, prepare the polenta, timing the cooking so that the polenta is done about when the chicken will be done. In a medium saucepan, bring the cold water to a boil. Add the olive oil and salt and whisk in the cornmeal. Bring to a simmer, stirring frequently. Cook for 20-30 minutes, stirring very often, until the grains of corn absorb the water and become tender. You may want to cover the polenta for the last 10 minutes of cooking and turn down the heat to medium-low if it looks like the water is absorbing quickly. You should have enough water, just give it the time it needs to cook. This is the reason I ask you to buy coarse cornmeal, because the finer ground cornmeal absorbs water very quickly and gets lumpy. Stir in the herbs, butter and cheese until well mixed. Taste for salt.

   To serve, ladle the polenta into serving bowls and top with a piece of the chicken with a lot of the pan juices.

HINT   Simply smash the garlic cloves with the side of a knife—do not mince them. The point is to release the garlic oil into the braise and leave the clove fairly well intact so that it can be eaten whole. This is delicious!

THIS DISH IS CALLED

Gallo Vecchio al Limone in Tuscany. *Gallo vecchio* literally means "old rooster" and has become the colloquial term for braised chicken. This dish does not take too long to prepare, especially if you have your butcher cut the chickens into pieces for you. Notice how the vegetables are not really sautéed—they are added as the chicken pieces finish browning and then the liquids are poured over the top and the whole thing is covered and stewed slowly. This produces tender vegetables that are vibrant in color and packed with flavor.

joe simone

Chicken with Citrus Zest

THIS DISH IS COOKED

like classic Florentine grilled chicken, weighed down with a brick or heavy weight. But it's marinated with rosemary, lemon and orange zest — unconventional, tasty and easy.

faith willinger

SERVES 4 TO 6

1 (3½ pound) (1.6 kg) chicken, cut in half
2 tablespoons extra-virgin olive oil
2 teaspoons grated orange zest
2 teaspoons grated lemon zest

1 tablespoon chopped fresh rosemary
Fine sea salt and freshly ground black
   pepper to taste

METHOD With sharp kitchen scissors, cut away a strip of bones from the chicken's tail end to the neck, along the back of each chicken half. Cut away any of the breast bone and the wishbone on each half. Place the chicken halves, skin-side-up, on a cutting board. With another cutting board, whack the chicken to make it as flat as possible. Place the chicken in a large pyrex dish and sprinkle with the olive oil, orange and lemon zests, rosemary salt and pepper. Marinate in the refrigerator from 10 minutes to 24 hours.

    The day of serving, heat a cast-iron grill pan over medium-low heat. Cook the chicken, skin-side-up, for 20 minutes, using a brick wrapped in foil (or a heavy weight on a plate) to weigh it down. Remove the brick, turn the chicken, replace the brick and cook for 15 minutes, or until the chicken juices run clear when pricked with a fork.

Fish Fillets with Breadcrumbs and Fresh Herbs

SERVES 4

¾ cup good quality plain dried breadcrumbs
¼ cup finely minced fresh herbs, such as
   basil, parsley, thyme, or a mixture
1 egg
1½ pounds (750 g) fish fillets, such as
   haddock, hake, cod, snapper, or flounder

¼ cup extra-virgin olive oil
2 garlic cloves
Lemon wedges, for garnish
Sea salt and pepper to taste

METHOD Mix the breadcrumbs and fresh herbs and spread over the bottom of a wide soup bowl. In another soup bowl, beat the egg well with a fork.

Cut the fish into 8 even pieces. Dunk each fish piece in the beaten egg, thoroughly covering the surface, then dredge it in the breadcrumbs, thoroughly covering all surfaces and pressing the crumbs so they coat the fish well. Place the breaded fish on a platter, cover with plastic wrap and refrigerate for 20-30 minutes. Chilling the fish will make the crumbs adhere better.

When ready to cook, in a large frying pan heat the olive oil over medium-high heat. Crush the garlic cloves with the flat blade of a knife, add to the hot oil and brown well. Remove and discard the garlic. Add the fish pieces to the hot, garlic-flavored oil and fry quickly, about 5 minutes to each side. The fish are thoroughly cooked when the outside is brown and the inside is opaque throughout. Sprinkle with the salt and pepper and serve with the lemon wedges.

THIS IS ONE OF THE **simplest recipes I know, but to make it even easier, you can do the egg-and-breadcrumb treatment several hours ahead and leave the fish fillets in the refrigerator until you're ready to cook. Then it's just a question of ten minutes at the stove and dinner is ready.**

nancy harmon jenkins

Seafood Packets

its ease as much as for its flavor
—ease of preparation and
clean-up, too! It may be varied
in many ways: instead of the
tomato, pepper and fresh herbs,
for instance, try a combination
of lemon zest, capers and green
or black olives. Although the
recipe serves one, it is easily
expanded to serve four, six
or more.

nancy harmon jenkins

SERVES 1

1¼ teaspoons extra-virgin olive oil
1 (4-5 ounce) (115-150 g) piece of swordfish
  or boneless fillet of sea bass, snapper,
  salmon, or haddock
¼ potato, diced
1 green onion, sliced diagonally
Pinch of finely minced garlic
1 thick slice of red, ripe tomato,
  seeded and diced

3 or 4 long thin strips of sweet red
  or yellow bell pepper
1 teaspoon finely chopped fresh herbs,
  such as dill, basil, chervil, chives, or
  a combination
1 teaspoon freshly squeezed lemon juice
Sea salt and freshly ground black pepper
  to taste

METHOD   Tear off a square of heavy-duty aluminum foil large enough to make a loose packet around the fish and the vegetables. Smear about ¼ teaspoon of the oil on the foil and set the fish in the middle.

Bring a small pot of water to a boil and throw in the potato dice. Return to a boil and cook for 4-5 minutes, until the potato is just tender, then drain immediately.

Arrange the parboiled potato, green onions, garlic, tomato and pepper strips on top of the fish. Sprinkle with the herbs, the remaining oil, the lemon juice and salt and pepper to taste. Pull up the sides of the foil and seal to make a loose but tightly closed packet. The packets may be prepared well ahead of time and refrigerated, but allow time to bring them back to room temperature before cooking.

When you're ready to cook, preheat the oven to 425°F (220°C). Set the packet on a baking sheet and bake until the fish and vegetables are done, about 20-25 minutes. Serve immediately in their packets, breaking each one open at the table to release the fragrance.

Seafood Packets

Steamed Mussels in White Wine with Garlic and Parsley

THERE WAS A TIME WHEN

mussels were confounding to

home cooks since they

required laborious cleaning.

Now, with clean, cultivated

mussels widely available, the

chore has been taken out of

mussel preparation and has

made this delicious seafood

something that should be part

of every cook's repertoire.

nancy harmon jenkins

SERVES 4

1 onion, finely chopped
4 garlic cloves, finely chopped
¼ cup extra-virgin olive oil
1 pound (450 g) very ripe tomatoes,
   peeled, seeded and chopped
½ cup dry white wine

1 bay leaf
1½ pounds (750 g) fresh mussels
½ cup finely minced fresh Italian parsley
½ cup fresh breadcrumbs
Sea salt and freshly ground black pepper
   to taste

METHOD   In the bottom of a deep heavy kettle or stockpot large enough to hold all the mussels, mix together the onion, garlic and 2 tablespoons of the olive oil. Cook over medium-low heat until the vegetables are very soft. Add the chopped tomatoes, wine, bay leaf and salt and pepper to taste, cover and cook until the sauce is somewhat thickened, about 10 minutes.

While the sauce is cooking, clean the mussels by rubbing the shells under running water. Discard any that are gaping or that feel suspiciously heavy, an indication that they are full of sand. Use a sharp paring knife to remove any beards that cling to the shells.

When the sauce has thickened, add the cleaned mussels to the pan, stirring with a wooden spoon to mix well. Raise the heat slightly and cook for 10 minutes, or until the shells have opened, indicating that the mussels are done. Discard any mussels that refuse to open after 10 minutes.

While the mussels are cooking, in another small frying pan set over medium heat, toast the breadcrumbs in the remaining 2 tablespoons of olive oil for about 3 minutes, or until they are golden.

Remove the cooked mussels from the pan and transfer to a serving platter or bowl. Stir the parsley into the sauce and then pour the hot simmering sauce over the mussels in the serving dish. Sprinkle with the toasted breadcrumbs and serve immediately, with plenty of paper napkins for wiping saucy fingers.

Steamed Mussels in White Wine with Garlic and Parsley

Pan Fried Sole Dipped in Parmesan and Breadcrumbs with Lemon and Escarole

MY FISHMONGER GETS

daybeat native sole every day. "Dayboat" means that the fishing boat goes out in the morning and comes back to port in the afternoon with its catch. This is in contrast to most large commercial fishing boats which will set to sea and return several days or weeks later with their catch iced down for a long period of time. I try to only buy dayboat fish because I know that it is fresher and tastes better and I like to think that I am supporting my local economy. If you do not live near a fishing port, by all means purchase whatever looks and smells fresh to you. And you could substitute any other mild fish for this dish — for example a super fresh brook trout would work well here.

joe simone

SERVES 4

¾ cup all-purpose flour
¼ cup freshly grated Parmigiano
  Reggiano cheese
1 heaping tablespoon chopped fresh parsley
1 cup dried breadcrumbs
2 eggs beaten with 2 tablespoons water
1½ pounds (750 g) very fresh fillet of sole

1 head escarole, washed and cut into
  ½ inch (1.5 cm) squares
2 tablespoons freshly squeezed lemon juice
½ cup plus 2 tablespoons extra-virgin
  olive oil
Kosher or sea salt to taste
Lemon slices, for garnish

METHOD   Line a baking sheet with wax paper. Place the flour in a small bowl. In another bowl, combine the Parmigiano Reggiano cheese, parsley and breadcrumbs. Set the bowl with the flour, next to the cheese mixture, and next to the bowl with the egg and water. Season the sole fillets lightly with salt and then bread them: dip them first in the flour, then in the egg wash and finally in the breadcrumb mixture. Place on the prepared baking sheet.

Heat a large skillet over medium heat. When hot, add the ½ cup of olive oil and then sauté the sole fillets until they are golden brown and crisp on both sides, about 2-3 minutes per side. Transfer to a warm serving platter.

Heat a heavy-duty skillet over high heat. When hot, add the remaining 2 tablespoons of olive oil and the escarole. Cook until the escarole wilts, about 3 minutes. Season with a little salt, add the lemon juice and cook for 1 minute. Serve the escarole with the sole, passing the pepper mill and a plate of sliced lemons at the table.

INGREDIENTS TIP   The Italians frown on the general idea of fish and cheese, but the grated Parmigiano adds a layer of complexity and I believe makes this dish stand out for its delicious simplicity.

Swordfish Medallions with Lemon, Capers and Sage

SERVES 4

4 very fresh (5 ounce) (150 g) swordfish
   cutlets, ¼ inch (6 mm) thick
2 tablespoons extra-virgin olive oil
1 heaping tablespoon capers, well rinsed
1 tablespoon minced fresh sage leaves

2 tablespoons freshly squeezed lemon juice
2 tablespoons dry white wine
1 tablespoon very cold unsalted butter
Kosher or sea salt to taste

METHOD   Season the swordfish with a little salt. Heat a skillet large enough to hold all of the swordfish in one layer. Add the olive oil and the fish and cook for 1 minute. Add the capers and sage. Turn the fish over and pour in the lemon juice and white wine. Cook until the swordfish is just cooked through, about 1 minute. Transfer the swordfish to a warm serving platter.

In the same skillet, raise the heat to high and add the cold butter. Cook and stir until the butter melts and a nice sauce is formed. Immediately pour the sauce over the swordfish and serve.

INGREDIENTS TIP   Although I like to use fresh sage in this recipe, you can substitute fresh parsley. I like the Italian flat-leaf variety.

THIS IS REALLY A VERSION of picatta—that overdone preparation mostly used with veal or chicken. When done correctly, with good quality capers that are rinsed very well, this preparation is divine. My fishmonger will cut the swordfish into nice uniform cutlets. I think that you should challenge yours to do the same. I am very careful about purchasing swordfish. I like to visually see a healthy translucent sheen to the swordfish and I always smell any fish I purchase to be sure that it has no "off" odors—a sure sign that the fish is old. The preparation of this dish is so simple and quick that you will find yourself making this dish often!

joe simone

Eggplant Parmesan

THIS RECIPE WAS TAUGHT

to me by Giovanna of Trattoria Pendemonio in Florence. I have already spoken of Giovanna and I must say that whenever I am in Florence her restaurant is the first place I stop—it is like going home for me. Note that the eggplant is dredged in flour and not breaded with breadcrumbs. The secret here is to drain the eggplant well and dry it carefully on paper toweling before dipping it in the flour. Also, I like to use peanut oil to fry my eggplant. When you fry, be sure not to crowd the pan and also make sure that each piece turns a deep golden brown.

joe simone

SERVES 4 TO 6

2 (1½ pound) (600 g) eggplants, preferably the Sicilian variety

1 cup all-purpose flour or more if needed

Vegetable oil, to fry the eggplant

1½ cups freshly grated Parmigiano Reggiano cheese

2 cups tomato sauce

Kosher or sea salt to taste

METHOD   Wash the eggplant and pat dry. Cut into ½ inch (1.5 cm) disks, with the skin on, and sprinkle with salt. Transfer to a colander, set in the sink, and let drain for at least 45 minutes and up to 2 hours.

When the eggplant has drained, pat each piece dry. Heat the vegetable oil in a heavy-duty skillet. Dip each eggplant disk into the flour and fry in batches until golden brown and crispy, about 8 minutes per batch. Drain the cooked eggplant on paper towels.

Preheat the oven to 375°F (190°C). Spoon a small amount of the tomato sauce across the bottom of a 9 x 9 x 2 inch (23 x 23 x 5 cm) baking dish, or any ovenproof dish that is similar in size. Arrange a layer of the cooked eggplant over the sauce. Spoon over a little tomato sauce and sprinkle with the grated Parmigiano Reggiano cheese. Arrange another layer of the eggplant and continue with the sauce, cheese and eggplant until you use all of the eggplant. Top with more of the sauce and cheese. Bake in the preheated oven until the casserole is hot and top is crispy, about 25 minutes. Remove from the oven and let rest for 5 minutes before serving.

HINT   This casserole can be made early in the day and then cooked in the oven when you are ready to serve it, or you can cook it ahead of time and eat it at room temperature.

INGREDIENTS TIP   *Joe's Tomato Sauce* (see recipe on page 97) accompanies this recipe quite well.

Joe's Tomato Sauce

MAKES ABOUT 3 CUPS

2 tablespoons extra-virgin olive oil

1 teaspoon minced garlic

1 heaping tablespoon fresh basil leaves, chopped

28 oz. (800 g) canned plum tomatoes in juice

1 teaspoon kosher salt or to taste

Freshly ground black pepper to taste

1 teaspoon granulated sugar

METHOD   Over a medium-high flame, heat the olive oil and garlic in a saucepan large enough to hold all of the ingredients. When the garlic sizzles and becomes fragrant add the basil, stir for 20 seconds until the basil becomes fragrant and then add the can of tomatoes. Simply open the can and pour it in. Immediately add the salt, pepper and sugar.

Bring to the boil, stirring often. Once boiling, reduce the heat to a simmer and cook, stirring occasionally, for 25-35 minutes, until the tomatoes have broken down and the sauce begins to thicken.

Pass the sauce through the food mill (or purée in a blender or use an immersion blender) and adjust the salt—you should not have to add more sugar.

HINT   The sugar may be omitted if desired. I find that the small amount of sugar counteracts any bitterness or excess acidity of the tomatoes.

INGREDIENTS TIP   I prefer Muir Glen Organic peeled tomatoes available in most stores on either coast. If these are unavailable, search out whole, peeled Roma tomatoes packed in juice. Do not use tomatoes with seasonings other than perhaps basil.

THIS IS A SIMPLE, all-purpose tomato sauce—perfect for a simple pasta or as an ingredient to many recipes. This sauce is so simple to prepare that there is no reason to purchase commercially prepared tomato sauce!

If you have an abundance of fresh, ripe tomatoes, cut them into pieces and proceed—making sure that you use the food mill to remove the skins.

joe simone

Fried Eggs with Parmigiano Reggiano

SERVES 2

4 tablespoons extra-virgin olive oil or butter (if you must)

4 large fresh eggs

Sea salt and freshly ground black pepper to taste

¼ cup freshly grated Parmigiano Reggiano cheese

Rustic country-style bread

METHOD   Drizzle 2 tablespoons of the olive oil into a nonstick skillet over medium heat. Gently fry the eggs until barely set, about 5 minutes. Sprinkle with the salt, pepper, cheese and the remaining oil. Cover and cook for 1 minute or until the egg whites are set. Serve immediately with slices of the bread.

ALWAYS ON THE MENU at my home—the addition of a sprinkle of Parmigiano does wonders for eggs. Mopping up the sauce with chunks of bread is considered good form.

faith willinger

Sautéed Turkey Cutlets with Tuna and Caper Mayonnaise

MANY PEOPLE HAVE

heard of the classic dish
Veal Tonatto. Well this is an
updated version made with
the breast of a turkey that is
sliced, lightly breaded and
then sautéed in olive oil. The
tonatto, or tuna mayonnaise,
may seem a bit strange but
rest assured that it is delicious.
If you have any leftovers this
makes an excellent turkey
sandwich with tonatto and
perhaps some arugula. I think
that this would be a perfect
addition to a summer buffet.

joe simone

SERVES 4 TO 6

1 pound (450 g) boneless, skinless turkey
   breast, uncooked
2 eggs beaten with 2 tablespoons water
½ cup all-purpose flour
1/4 cup freshly grated Parmigiano
   Reggiano cheese
1 cup dried breadcrumbs
1 tablespoon chopped fresh parsley leaves
1 cup extra-virgin olive oil

The Tonatto

1 (5 ounce) (150 g) can tuna, packed in oil,
   preferably Italian
1 tablespoon freshly squeezed lemon juice
1 tablespoon capers, rinsed well
½ cup mayonnaise
Kosher or sea salt to taste

METHOD   Cut the turkey breast against the grain into 6 pieces of about the same size. Line a smooth working surface with plastic wrap and arrange the turkey cutlets over the plastic. Cover the turkey with another sheet of plastic wrap and then gently pound the turkey until they are uniformly thin, about ¼ inch (6 mm) thick. If you have a nice butcher, ask him to do this for you! Season lightly with salt and set aside.

In a medium bowl, mix the cheese, breadcrumbs and parsley until well combined. Place next to a bowl with the flour, another bowl with the egg mixture and then finally the breadcrumb mixture. Bread the cutlets by dipping them first in the flour, then the egg mixture and finally the breadcrumb mixture. Set them on a clean platter or baking sheet in one layer.

Heat ½ cup of the olive oil in a large skillet until very hot. Fry the cutlets without overlapping until crispy and golden brown. You will probably have to fry in batches, depending on the size of your skillet. As soon as the cutlets turn golden brown, transfer them to a double thickness of paper towels. Keep warm while you prepare the tuna mayonnaise.

Drain the tuna of its excess oil and transfer to a food processor or blender. Pulse several times to break down the tuna. Add the lemon juice and capers and process for 20 seconds. Add the mayonnaise and, with the machine running, drizzle in the remaining ½ cup olive oil. Taste the mayonnaise and correct the seasonings with salt and additional lemon juice if needed.

To serve, arrange the warm cutlets on a platter and top with the tonatto.

INGREDIENTS TIP   Do search out the Italian style tuna packed in oil. It is much better for this recipe. But if you cannot find any you could substitute the water packed variety, drained well and then add a bit more olive oil to compensate for the dryness of the water packed tuna.

Sautéed Turkey Cutlets with Tuna and Caper Mayonnaise

Herbal Marinade for Beef, Pork, Lamb, or Chicken

YIELDS ENOUGH MARINADE FOR ABOUT 1½ POUNDS (750 G) OF MEAT.

½ cup extra-virgin olive oil

¼ cup aged red wine vinegar or freshly squeezed orange juice

2 garlic cloves, finely chopped

1 teaspoon finely chopped fresh rosemary, needles only

1 teaspoon finely chopped fresh thyme, leaves only

1 teaspoon finely chopped green onion tops or fresh chives

1 tablespoon finely chopped fresh Italian parsley, leaves only

Sea salt and freshly ground black pepper to taste

METHOD Place all the ingredients in a jar, cover with a tight-fitting lid and shake vigorously.

HINT Marinde small pieces of meat, such as chops or chicken pieces, for a few hours. Larger cuts of beef or pork roasts for instance, may be marinated for up to 24 hours in the refrigerator.

VARY THIS MIXTURE

depending on what herbs are available in your market. You could use a little sage, for instance, in place of the chives; or lovage or chervil instead of the rosemary. Whatever your selection, be sure to set aside a sprig or two to use as a garnish with the dish.

nancy harmon jenkins

Herbal Marinade for Beef, Pork, Lamb or Chicken
Grilled New Potatoes, see recipe on page 110.

Braised Pork with Black Olives and Polenta

SERVES 4 TO 6

The Pork

4 tablespoons extra-virgin olive oil

1½ tablespoons white wine vinegar

¾ cup dry white wine

1 large garlic clove, slivered

1 tablespoon minced fresh thyme leaves

2 bay leaves

2 pounds (900 g) boneless pork butt or
    pork loin

1 pound (450 g) Spanish onions, sliced into
    thin julienne

2 tablespoons unsalted butter

1 cup pitted black olives, preferably Gaeta

Kosher or sea salt and freshly ground black
    pepper to taste

The Polenta

3½ cups cold water

1 tablespoon salt or to taste

1 tablespoon extra-virgin olive oil

1 cup cornmeal, preferably Gary's organic
    stoneground coarse

1 tablespoon unsalted butter

¼ cup freshly grated Parmigiano Reggiano
    cheese

2 tablespoons chopped herbs, such as Italian
    parsley, chives, or oregano, etc.

METHOD   For the pork, combine the first 8 ingredients in a deep bowl or dish to make a marinade. Add the pork and onions, cover with plastic wrap and marinate for 2 hours in a cool dark place or refrigerate overnight. Let come back to room temperature before proceeding.

Discard the bay leaves from the marinating pork. Melt the butter in a large ovenproof casserole and add the pork, reserving the onions and marinade. Brown the meat on all sides. Add the onions, marinade and the olives. Reduce the heat and simmer, covered, until the meat is cooked through and is tender, about 45 minutes to 1 hour.

While the meat is cooking, prepare the polenta, timing the preparation so that it's done when you're ready to serve the pork. Bring the water to a boil. Add the boiling water to the upper part of a double boiler set over simmering water. Whisk in the salt, olive oil and polenta. Stir well, cover and set the double boiler over medium heat. Cook 15 minutes, whisking occasionally, until the mixture begins to thicken. Remove from the heat and hold until the pork is cooked.

When the pork is cooked, finishing the polenta by transferring it to a skillet set over medium high heat. If the polenta is too firm, add a bit of water. Simmer until you have the proper consistency. Add the butter, herbs and cheese and stir to incorporate. Taste for salt.

To serve, divide the polenta among serving plates. Slice the pork into serving pieces and serve over the polenta, spoon some of the olive sauce over all.

HINT   The braised pork is actually better if made one or two days in advance! To reheat the pork, bake it, covered with plastic wrap and aluminum foil, in a 325°F (170°C) oven for 1 hour.

FOR THIS RECIPE, I LIKE

to use boneless pork butt or

shoulder versus the pork loin.

I find that the dish is more suc-

culent if made with less lean

meat. This is such a rustic dish

and was inspired from a

Ligurian recipe by my friend

Fred Plotkin. Please do not use

canned pitted black olives since

they have little or no flavor.

Although I love the flavor of

the corn with the pork sauce,

you could serve the pork over

mashed potatoes.

joe simone

Braised Pork with Black Olives and Polenta

CHAPTER FOUR

Side Dishes

THE WORD ITALIANS use for side dish is *contorno*. Its non-culinary meaning is "edge." The concept is that the main course's accompaniment is designed to fill the edge of the plate. In addition, it serves to fill the "edge" of the diner's appetite.

The side dish should enhance the main course, not be in conflict with it. It should help bring out subtleties of flavor that would be missed without it. The simple, delicious side dishes in this chapter will do just that.

Caponata

THIS IS A GREAT FAVORITE

on Italian-American tables. Although expensive ingredients like pine nuts and raisins can be part of a caponata, the basic mix is made with seasonal vegetables — eggplants, onions, bell peppers and tomatoes — when they're at their tasty best and cheapest. If you've only tried commercial canned caponata, I think you'll be surprised at how much more flavorful this is, especially if you use a well-flavored extra-virgin olive oil for cooking. It's a delicious summertime antipasto to take the place of salad or a vegetable to accompany plainly grilled meat or fish.

nancy harmon jenkins

SERVES 4 TO 6

- 2 pounds (900 g) eggplant, unpeeled and cut into 1¼ inch (4 cm) fingers
- ½ pound (225 g) sweet red or yellow bell peppers
- ¼ cup extra-virgin olive oil or more if necessary
- 1 pound (450 g) yellow onions, peeled, halved and thinly sliced
- 1 pound (450 g) fresh red, ripe tomatoes, peeled, seeded and chopped
- ¼ cup red wine vinegar
- 1-2 teaspoons sugar
- 2 stalks celery, coarsely chopped
- ¼ cup coarsely chopped, pitted green olives
- 1 tablespoon capers, rinsed if salted
- ¼ cup fresh basil leaves
- Coarse sea salt and sugar to taste

METHOD   Place the eggplant fingers in a colander and sprinkle with the sea salt. Set a plate on top of the eggplant, weight it down and set aside to drain for an hour or so. When ready to use, rinse the salt away under cold running water and dry the eggplant fingers with paper towel.

While the eggplant is draining, pierce the peppers with a long-handled fork and roast them over a gas flame or charcoal embers. If necessary, place them on a baking sheet under an oven broiler. Cook until the outside skins are black and blistered. Rub the blackened skin away and, when the peppers are clean, slice them lengthwise into ½ inch (1.5 cm) strips. Discard the seeds, stems and inner membranes. Set aside.

In a shallow saucepan large enough to hold all the ingredients, heat the oil over medium-high until it casts a blue haze. Add the eggplant fingers and sauté briefly, 2-3 minutes to a side, until they are golden brown. Remove and set aside.

Add more oil to the pan at this point if necessary — eggplant often absorbs a great deal of oil. Add the onion slices to the pan and cook over medium-low heat until the onions are soft and starting to turn golden. Do not let the onions brown.

While the onions are cooking, in a separate pan combine the tomatoes, sugar and vinegar. Cook over medium heat, stirring frequently, until the tomatoes have turned into a sweet-sour marmalade, about 15 minutes. Remove from the heat and stir in the celery, olives and capers. Add the mixture to the pan with the onions, stir in the eggplant and pepper strips, then cook on very low heat, simmering gently, until the flavors are well combined and the mixture is thick, about 5-10 minutes. Immediately remove from the heat and taste for seasoning, adding more salt, pepper, or sugar if desired. Stir in the basil leaves and set aside to rest. Serve only when the caponata is at room temperature or a little above.

Gratin of Braised Fennel

SERVES 4 TO 6

½ cup chicken, meat, or vegetable stock
4 bulbs of fennel
1½ cups extra-virgin olive oil

4 tablespoons freshly grated Parmigiano
    Reggiano cheese
Sea salt and freshly ground black pepper
    to taste

METHOD   Preheat the oven to 325°F (170°C). In a small saucepan, simmer the stock until reduced by half to concentrate the flavors, about 5 minutes.

While the stock is simmering, bring a large pot of lightly salted water to a rolling boil. Cut each fennel bulb in half lengthwise and trim the root ends. Very large fennel bulbs may be cut into quarters. Cut off any stalks that protrude more than an inch (2.5 cm) or so above the bulbs. Drop the trimmed fennel into the boiling water and simmer for 7 minutes, then drain, refresh in cold water, and drain again.

Use a little of the olive oil to grease the bottom and sides of a 9 x 13 inch (23 x 33 cm) pan or an ovenproof dish, just large enough to hold the fennel, and suitable to bring to the table for serving. Arrange the fennel in the dish, spoon with the reduced stock, sprinkle with the salt and pepper and drizzle liberally with the remaining olive oil.

Cover the dish with aluminum foil and bake in the preheated oven until the fennel can be pierced easily with a fork, about 30 minutes. Remove the foil and sprinkle the fennel with the cheese. Raise the oven temperature to 500°F (260°C) and return the pan, uncovered, to the hot oven to cook for 10-15 minutes, or until the cheese melts and the fennel starts to brown. Serve immediately.

INGREDIENTS TIP   Fennel is also known as Florence fennel and, for some reason, in many supermarket produce departments (but nowhere else) it's called anise. When buying fennel, look for firm, heavy, white bulbs. The tops, which are partially removed for this recipe, should have a fresh, green look.

IN THIS SIMPLE RECIPE the fennel is first braised, then sprinkled with cheese to make a gratin topping. Other vegetables that could be used include leeks, Brussels sprouts, Jerusalem artichokes and carrots.

nancy harmon jenkins

Red Peppers Baked with Olive Paste and Red Wine

FABIO PICCHI MENTIONED

this dish to me and I fell in love with it. It's no longer on the menu at Cibreo but is at my home.

faith willinger

SERVES 4

2 red bell peppers
2 whole salt-packed anchovies
2 garlic cloves, peeled
2 tablespoons salt-packed capers, rinsed well

1 tablespoon fresh chopped parsley
¼ cup black olive paste
2 tablespoons extra-virgin olive oil
1 cup red wine

METHOD   Preheat the oven to 400°F (200°C).

Slice the red peppers in half, leaving the stems intact. Remove the seeds and white pith.

Using an immersion mixer or food processor, process the anchovies, garlic, capers, parsley, olive paste and oil until smooth. Divide the mixture into the four pepper halves. Transfer to a small baking dish that will fit the four peppers in one layer. Pour the red wine into the dish and bake for 45-55 minutes or until brown. Serve at room temperature.

HINT   If you can't find olive paste you can make your own. Sauté about ⅓ cup of medium-sized California black olives in 2 tablespoons of extra-virgin olive oil for about 2 minutes on medium-high heat. Transfer to a food processor and process until you have a smooth paste.

Red Peppers Baked with Olive Paste and Red Wine

Grilled New Potatoes with Garlic and Herbs

USE WHATEVER COMES

up—in the garden or the

farmer's market—for the

fresh herbs in this recipe.

Rosemary is delicious with

potatoes, but so are unusual

herbs like lovage or oregano.

Very delicate herbs, like

chervil or tarragon, however,

may get lost in this dish. Save

them for a gentler treatment.

nancy harmon jenkins

SERVES 4 TO 6

24 small new potatoes, red or white,
   or a mixture
½ cup extra-virgin olive oil
¼ cup chopped fresh herbs, such as Italian
   parsley, basil, thyme, chives, or a mixture

2 garlic cloves, finely minced
Sea salt and freshly ground black
   pepper to taste

METHOD   Scrub the potatoes well. Transfer to a large saucepan, cover with water and bring to a boil over high heat. As soon as the water begins to boil, immediately reduce the heat and simmer for about 10 minutes or until the potatoes are slightly tender but not cooked all the way through. Drain immediately. When cool enough to handle, cut into halves and transfer to a bowl.

While the potatoes are simmering, in a small bowl whisk together the remaining ingredients until well mixed. Add half of the mixture to the cooled potatoes and toss well. Set the other half of the mixture aside.

On a charcoal grill, arrange a rack about 5 inches (13 cm) from the coals. Heat the coals until they are white. Place the potato halves, cut-side-down, on the grill and cook for about 10 minutes. They should not blacken, but should have cross-hatching grill marks from the grill on the cut sides. If the potatoes blacken, move the grilling rack a little farther away from the coals.

When the potatoes are done, transfer them to a clean bowl and immediately, while they're still hot, pour the remaining olive oil mixture over the top and toss well. Serve immediately.

Sautéed Spinach, Chard or Other Greens

SERVES 2 TO 4

2 pounds (900 g) spinach or other greens
¼ cup extra-virgin olive oil or more, if desired
1-2 garlic cloves, chopped

1 small dried hot red chili pepper, broken into pieces, or large pinch red pepper flakes, if desired
Freshly squeezed lemon juice to taste
Sea salt to taste

METHOD Carefully wash and pick over the greens in several changes of water to get rid of any soil, dust and wilted leaves. Place the greens, with the water clinging to their leaves, in a large pot and set over medium heat. The greens should cook in their own juices plus the rinsing water, but tougher greens, such as collards, may need the addition of ¼ cup of water. Add salt to taste, cover and cook the greens, stirring occasionally, to mix the cooked greens on the bottom with the as yet uncooked greens toward the top. Cooking time will vary, but spinach should be done in about 10 minutes. Collards are traditionally cooked for a very long time, but they are actually done in about 20 minutes and, for nontraditionalists, they have a fresher taste thereby.

When the greens are done, drain thoroughly in a colander. Use a metal spatula or a chopping blade to chop the greens coarsely right in the colander—this will help drain away excess water. As soon as the greens are cool enough to handle, remove from the colander, squeezing to release more water, and transfer to a chopping board. Chop coarsely.

Pour the oil into a large frying pan set on medium heat and gently cook the garlic and chili pepper, if desired, until the garlic is soft, about 5 minutes. Add the chopped greens, stirring and tossing in the garlicky oil until the greens are thoroughly warmed, about 5 minutes. Remove from the heat and taste, adding salt, pepper and lemon juice, if desired. Serve immediately.

THIS RECIPE IS A traditional way to cook spinach, chard or broccoli rabe (rapini) but it works well with many other types of greens, including collards, bok choy or Chinese flowering broccoli. Mature chard and collards should have the tough central ribs removed, then the remaining leafy parts slivered before cooking. Broccoli rabe often needs very careful trimming to get rid of tough stalks and yellowing leaves.

nancy harmon jenkins

Vegetable Medley

AT THE HEIGHT OF EACH

season, except perhaps deep midwinter in the North, vegetables in farmer's markets and well-stocked produce sections are at their peak of flavor and texture. This is the time to assemble a medley of vegetables: it might be peas, morels, asparagus, and ramps or wild onions in springtime; tomatoes, sweet peppers, corn and eggplants in summer; or squashes, onions, leeks, carrots and dried beans as autumn drifts into winter. Use your own judgment, based on what's available and remember the Golden Rule of vegetable cookery: restraint. In other words, if two or three vegetables are wonderful together, six or eight will represent nothing more than a confusion of tastes.

nancy harmon jenkins

SERVES 6

¼ cup extra-virgin olive oil
2 tablespoons finely minced yellow onion
6 garlic cloves, peeled but left whole
12 small ripe cherry tomatoes, left whole
1 celery stalk, coarsely chopped
1 bay leaf
¼ cup coarsely chopped fresh Italian parsley
¼ cup chicken or vegetable stock or more,
    if necessary

1 pound (450 g) young slender green beans,
    tops and tails removed and cut into 2 inch
    (5 cm) lengths, if very long
¼ pound (225 g) shiitake mushrooms, brushed
    clean and sliced into ¼ inch (6 mm) pieces
Juice of ½ lemon
Sea salt and freshly ground black pepper
    to taste

METHOD   In a broad, straight-sided saucepan set over medium-low heat, pour 2 tablespoons of the olive oil. Add the onion, garlic and tomatoes and cook, tossing occasionally, until the vegetables are sizzling lightly in the oil, about 7-8 minutes. Add the celery, bay leaf, half the parsley and 2 tablespoons of the stock and stir well. Cover the pot tightly, lower the heat and let the vegetables sweat until the tomatoes become soft, about 10 minutes. From time to time, remove the cover and stir gently. If the liquid starts to evaporate, add a few tablespoons of water or stock.

Add the green beans and remaining 2 tablespoons of the stock, stirring to mix well. Cover and cook for 10 minutes, or until the beans are tender. Stir occasionally, and if the liquid starts to evaporate, add a few tablespoons of water or stock.

While the beans cook, pour the remaining 3 tablespoons of olive oil into a frying pan set over medium heat and fry the mushrooms until they have rendered their juices. Add the lemon juice, raise the heat to medium-high, and cook until most of the liquid has evaporated. Transfer the mushrooms to the beans and tomatoes, along with the remaining parsley, and cook for 5 minutes to amalgamate the flavors. If there is too much liquid in the pan, raise the heat and tilt the pan to boil it away rapidly. There should be no more than a few tablespoons of syrupy liquid in the bottom pan, just enough to coat the vegetables. Serve immediately.

HINT   Although this dish is best served immediately, if necessary, it can be prepared in advance, then transferred, with the liquid, to a shallow gratin dish or ovenproof pan and covered with aluminum foil. Reheat in the oven for 10-15 minutes before serving.

Vegetable Medley

Soufiko Ikarian Style

SERVES 4 TO 6

1 large yellow onion, halved and thinly sliced
⅓-½ cup extra-virgin olive oil
1 big chunk (about 2 pounds (900 g) of hard
    winter squash, such as calabash or
    Hubbard, cut into narrow chunks

3 large ripe plum tomatoes, peeled and sliced
1 small dried hot chili pepper, crumbled
3 fresh green bell peppers, sliced in wedges
Sea salt and freshly ground black pepper
    to taste

METHOD   Pour 2 tablespoons of the olive oil into a large frying pan set on medium heat and sauté the onion very gently just until it starts to soften, about 7-8 minutes. Do not let it brown. Add salt to taste, then the remainder of the olive oil. Add the squash and stir well to coat the pieces with the oil.

Continue cooking, uncovered, without stirring, for about 20 minutes, while the squash absorbs the flavors of the onion and olive oil. Arrange the tomato slices over the top. Add the dried and fresh green peppers, pushing them down into the mixture. Cook for 20 minutes, stirring gently from time to time, or until the squash and green peppers are tender. When done, taste for seasoning, remove from the heat and serve immediately.

THIS DISH FROM THE Greek island of Ikaria, was made for me by Argyro Koutsoutis in her Queens, New York, kitchen. The same preparation works well with many other vegetables. In summer, Argyro sometimes substitutes fresh summer squash, like zucchini, yellow or crookneck squash, or even a mixture of summer squash and eggplant, for the hard winter squash. You may also substitute a fresh green jalapeño or serano chili for the dried red chili.

nancy harmon jenkins

Soufiko Ikarian Style

CHAPTER
FIVE

Breads and Pizzas

IN ITALY A very good person s described as "a piece of bread." This image reflects the inherent goodness of this common staple. There was a time, however, when bread was a luxury for many poor peasant families—the majority of the population. Their usual fare of beans and legumes was only occasionally enhanced by the deliciously satisfying flavor and texture of bread.

Perhaps it is in remembrance of this that Italians are so devoted to bread. It has a place at every meal: without bread they would not even consider eating a piece of cheese. At lunch and dinner, bread is used to make *la scarpetta*, "the slipper" used to sop up the left-over sauce from a dish of pasta, or to sponge the "little soup," *la zuppetta*, created by the olive oil, lemon juice, and pot liquor of cooked greens.

When the bread begins to dry, it is toasted and served with butter and preserves for breakfast. This toast is also used as a base for bruschetta, the traditional after-school snack. While there is still some life left in this precious food, it is used as the "rafts" in soup. In some regions, several-days-old bread is cubed, fried in olive oil, and sprinkled with grated cheese to create a simple meal. When the remainder of a loaf has turned as hard as a brick-bat, it still has use grated into bread crumbs.

The breads in this chapter range from simple and fancy hearth-breads to a magnificent loaf filled with black olives. All of them are sure to have the taste of real Italian bread and give the delicious, satisfying joy of home bread-making.

Flatbread from Nove Ligure
Focaccia alla Novese

THOUGH I HAVE NEVER
been to Nove Ligure near
Genoa, the home of this
wonderful focaccia, I tasted
it at the Slow Food confer-
ence I attended in Turin
in November, 1998. (Slow
Food is an international
association that promotes
artisanally made food
and food products throughout Europe.)

nick malgieri

SERVES 8

The Focaccia Dough
4 cups unbleached all-purpose flour
1½ teaspoons salt
2 tablespoons lard or oil for the dough
1½ cups warm tap water
1 envelope active dry yeast

For Finishing
6 tablespoons olive oil, divided
1 tablespoon kosher or other coarse salt

METHOD   To make the focaccia dough, place the flour and salt in a bowl and rub in the lard or oil by hand, rubbing the mixture between the palms of your hand to mix it. Place the water in a bowl and whisk in the yeast. Stir the yeast mixture into the flour mixture and continue to stir until a soft dough forms. Beat the dough for a few seconds to make it smoother, then cover the bowl with plastic wrap. Let the dough rise at room temperature for about an hour, or until it is double in bulk.

When the dough is risen, use half the oil to grease a 10 x 15 inch (25 cm x 38 cm) jelly roll pan. Scrape the dough out onto the pan and press it to fill the pan completely. If it resists, leave it for a few minutes, then press it into the pan. Cover loosely with plastic wrap and allow to rise until puffy and risen, about 45 minutes.

About 20 minutes before you intend to bake the focaccia, set a rack in the lower third of the oven and preheat to 450°F (230°C). Gently dimple the top of the focaccia using your fingertips, then drizzle with the remaining oil and sprinkle with the salt. Bake the focaccia until it is well colored on the top and bottom, about 25-30 minutes. Slide the focaccia to a rack to cool.

Serve the focaccia in squares as an hors d'oeuvre or as a bread at the table. This recipe makes one (10 x 15 inch) (25 cm x 38 cm) focaccia.

HINT   What distinguishes this focaccia is the presence of lard in the dough, which makes it a little more tender and rich. If you don't want to use lard, olive oil makes a good substitute.

Flatbread from Nove Ligure (Focaccia alla Novese) and Breadsticks from Piemonte (Grissini), see recipe on page 131.

Home-style Bread
Pane Casareccio

THIS HOMEMADE BREAD

is easy to prepare and

always gives beautiful

results. Fermenting the

sponge or biga overnight

gives better flavor and

texture to the bread.

nick malgieri

MAKES ONE LARGE ROUND LOAF

The Biga
1 cup tepid tap water
1 teaspoon active dry yeast
2 cups unbleached all-purpose flour

The Dough
All the biga (see left)
1 cup tepid tap water
1 teaspoon active dry yeast
3-3½ cups unbleached all-purpose flour
2½ teaspoons salt
Cornmeal, for the pan

METHOD For the biga, pour the water into a bowl and whisk in the yeast. Stir in the flour and cover the bowl with plastic wrap. Let the mixture ferment at room temperature for about 8 hours or overnight.

When you are ready to mix the bread dough, pour the water into the bowl of a heavy duty mixer fitted with the dough hook. Whisk in the yeast by hand, then stir in the risen biga with a rubber spatula. Use the same spatula to stir in the flour and salt. Place the dough on the mixer and mix on low speed for about 5 minutes, or until the dough is smooth and elastic. If the dough is too soft, beat in the remaining flour. Remove the bowl from the mixer and cover it with plastic wrap. Let the dough rise at room temperature until it is double in bulk, about an hour.

To shape the loaf, scrape the dough to a floured work surface and deflate it. Shape the dough into a sphere by tucking the edges in all around the bottom. Cover loosely with plastic wrap or a towel and allow to rise at room temperature for about an hour or so, or until double in bulk.

About 20 minutes before the loaf is fully risen, set a rack in the middle level of the oven and preheat to 400°F (200°C).

When the loaf is fully risen, place the loaf in the center of a cornmeal dusted pan. Use a sharp knife or razor to slash a cross in the top of the loaf. Immediately place the loaf in the oven. Bake until it reaches an internal temperature of about 200°F (180°C) for about 45-50 minutes. Cool the loaf on a rack.

Keep loosely covered at room temperature on the day the loaf is baked. Wrap in foil and freeze for longer storage.

Home-style Bread (Pane Casareccio)

Olive Bread

THIS BREAD WORKS BEST

with fairly dry olives, like the wrinkled ones called "oil-cured" (they aren't really oil cured at all), but in a pinch you can substitute small, black, brine-cured olives like the tasty ones from Gaeta or even Niçoise olives. Big juicy olives like Kalamatas will add too much liquid to the dough.

nancy harmon jenkins

YIELDS 2 LOAVES

1 teaspoon active dry yeast
3 cups warm water
5-6 cups unbleached all-purpose flour or more if necessary
1 teaspoon sea salt

A little extra-virgin olive oil, to grease the bowl
¼ cup pitted black olives, preferably "oil-cured"

METHOD   The night before you plan to bake the bread, in a large bowl, dissolve the yeast in 1½ cups of the warm water. Stir in 1½ cups of the flour. Stir with a wooden spoon until well mixed then cover with a damp towel or plastic wrap and set aside to rise in a cool place, between 60-70°F (15-20°C). This is called making a "sponge."

The day of baking, add the remaining 1½ cups warm water, salt and about 3½ cups of the remaining flour to the sponge. Don't feel you have to use all the flour. This is supposed to be quite a wet dough. Depending on the type of flour you're using, you may even have to use less. Sprinkle a little of the remaining flour on a large wooden board, transfer the sponge to the board, and knead very well for 10-15 minutes. The dough should feel smooth, elastic and satiny—bakers like to say "like a baby's bottom" or like the lobe of your ear. Rinse and dry the mixing bowl and spread a little of the olive oil thinly around the inside. Form the dough into a ball and turn it against the sides of the bowl to coat with the olive oil. Cover with a damp towel or plastic wrap and set aside to rise until doubled, about 2 hours.

When the dough has doubled, transfer it to a lightly floured board. Punch it down and spread it out to form a rough circle. Scatter the olives across the dough, roll it up to enclose the olives, then knead briefly, just enough to distribute the olives throughout the dough. Divide the dough into 2 pieces and shape into round or oblong loaves. Set the loaves on a large baking sheet about 2 inches (5 cm) from each other. Cover and let rise for 30 minutes.

Preheat the oven to 425°F (220°C). Just before putting the loaves in the oven, slash the tops several times with a knife. Bake until the bread is golden and crusty and feels hollow when you tap on it, about 35 minutes. Turn out onto a rack and leave for at least 2 hours to settle before cutting.

Olive Bread

Green Olive, Cheese and Ham Bread

SERVES 6 TO 8

½ cup extra-virgin olive oil
½ cup dry white wine
4 eggs
½ cup grated Gruyère cheese
½ cup pitted green olives

½ cup baked ham, diced
1 teaspoon baking powder
1 cup all-purpose flour
Salt and freshly ground black pepper

METHOD   Butter and lightly flour a 9 x 2 inch (23 x 5 cm) round cake pan. Preheat the oven to 375°F (190°C).

Combine the olive oil, wine and eggs in a mixing bowl and beat with a wire whisk just enough to mix well. Stir in the grated cheese, olives and ham.

In a small bowl, mix the baking powder with the flour, salt and pepper, then stir into the egg mixture. Using a spoon or a rubber spatula, mix everything well. Turn the mixture into the prepared cake pan and bake in the preheated oven for 45 minutes, or until the bread is thoroughly cooked and golden on the top. Turn it out on a cake rack and let cool slightly before cutting and serving.

A SLICE OF THIS RICHLY **satisfying bread from Provence makes a terrific breakfast. You'll notice a great deal of bubbling action from the olive oil when you remove the bread from the oven. Don't worry; it will settle down quickly.**

nancy harmon jenkins

Green Olive, Cheese and Ham Bread

Pizza Dough

¾ teaspoon active dry yeast

1 cup very warm water

2 cups unbleached all-purpose flour,
    plus more flour for kneading

1 cup soft pastry flour

1 teaspoon sea salt

1 teaspoon olive oil

I'VE ADDED A LITTLE pastry flour to this dough to make it approximate the kind of flour Neapolitan *pizzaioli* use. Otherwise, this is the classic: flour, salt, yeast and water, and just a little olive oil to rub on the inside of the bowl.

nancy harmon jenkins

METHOD In a medium measuring cup, dissolve the yeast in the very warm water. In a large bowl, combine the 2 flours, then pour them onto a wooden board. Make a hollow depression, or well, in the center. Add the salt and dissolved yeast into the well. Gradually, using your fingers, draw the flour into the liquid, mixing and blending well. Be careful not to break down the sides of the well.

When the ingredients are well amalgamated, start to knead the dough, sprinkling a little more flour on the board to keep it from sticking as needed. Knead for about 10 minutes or until the dough is springy and elastic. Shape the dough into a ball.

Lightly brush a large bowl with the olive oil. Transfer the dough to the bowl and cover with a damp towel or plastic wrap. Leave in a warm place to rise until it has doubled in volume, about 3 hours. The dough may be kept several hours longer with no damage.

When the dough is well risen, turn it out onto a floured board. Punch it down and knead briefly, just to get rid of the air holes. Your dough is ready to become your favorite pizza!

Pizza with Tomato Sauce, see recipe on page 129.
Neapolitan Carnival Pie (Pizza Rustica alla Napoletana),
see recipe on page 130.

Tomato Sauce for Pizza

THIS IS THE SIMPLEST, easiest, tastiest tomato sauce in the world. When tomatoes are in season (and only when they are in season in your neighborhood, not in Mexico or Florida), you may substitute an equivalent quantity of peeled, seeded, coarsely chopped fresh tomatoes. In that case, you will need to cook the sauce a little longer to reduce the tomatoes to a purée.

nancy harmon jenkins

YIELDS 2¼ CUPS

¼ cup extra-virgin olive oil
1 yellow onion, finely chopped
2-4 garlic cloves, finely chopped
28 ounces (800 g) canned plum tomatoes
1 small dried red chili pepper, if desired

1 tablespoon finely minced fresh Italian parsley or 10 big basil leaves, torn into bits or ½ teaspoon dried oregano
Sea salt and freshly ground black pepper to taste

METHOD   In a medium saucepan over medium to medium-low heat warm the olive oil. Add the onion and garlic and cook gently, stirring occasionally, until the vegetables are melted in the pan, about 8-10 minutes. Be careful not to brown them.

While the onion and garlic are cooking, pour the canned tomatoes into a sieve or a colander over a bowl. Remove and discard as much as you can of the tomato seeds, then break the tomatoes into small pieces using your hands. As soon as the onion and garlic are soft, add the tomato pieces and 1 cup of the tomato juice in the bowl. Bring to a simmer and cook gently, uncovered, for 15-20 minutes. If you're using the chili pepper and dried oregano, you should add it at this point.

The tomatoes will break down somewhat as they cook, or you can encourage this by breaking them up with a fork or the side of a spoon. The finished sauce should be thick and chunky, but not dry.

When the sauce is done, taste for salt and pepper if desired. Remove from the heat and stir in the fresh herbs, if using. If you used the chili pepper, remove and discard it at this point.

HINT   This sauce is intended for pizza, but it's just as good with pasta. If you don't use it all at once, it will keep in the refrigerator for up to a week, especially if you skin the surface with a thin layer of olive oil. It also freezes very nicely.

Pizza with Tomato Sauce

YIELDS 1 PIZZA

1 recipe Pizza Dough (see page 126)

A little cornmeal, if you're using a peel

Extra-virgin olive oil, as needed

1 recipe Tomato Sauce for Pizza
(see page 128)

Your choice of toppings, for examples:

Fresh whole milk mozzarella cheese

Freshly grated Parmigiano Reggiano cheese

Crumbled fresh goat cheese

Anchovies, salted or oil-cured

Torn basil leaves

Grilled or roasted sweet bell peppers

Sliced red onions

Grilled Ratatouille (see page 31)

Pitted black or green olives

Three Onion Confit (see Three Onion Tart
on page 36)

METHOD   Preheat the oven to 500°F (260°C) or as hot as your oven will go. If you're using a baking stone, put the cold stone into the cold oven and preheat for at least 30 minutes in order to heat the stone all the way through. If you're not using a baking stone, just heat the oven until it reaches the correct temperature.

Divide the pizza dough in half and roll each half into a ball. Set 1 ball aside, covered with a damp towel. On a lightly floured board, pat the other ball into a thick circle. Now, working quickly with a rolling pin, roll it out on the board to about ½-¼ inch (3-6 mm) thick. If you're using a baking stone, sprinkle a peel with cornmeal and set the dough circle on the peel. If you're using a baking sheet, oil it lightly and set the dough circle on it.

Smear about ¾ cup of the tomato sauce over the dough, coming to ¼ inch (6 mm) of the edge. Add one or more of the toppings. Do not be overly extravagant—this is one case where less is truly more. If you were to use *Grilled Ratatouille*, for instance, that would be enough in and of itself. You could make a *Pizza Margherita* just by topping the tomato sauce with a little crumbled mozzarella, a few basil leaves, and a tablespoon or two of grated Parmigiano Reggiano. Or you could use the Three Onion Confit from the *Three Onion Tart* with a few coarsely chopped anchovies and black olives scattered over.

When everything is ready to go into the oven, work very quickly. If you're using a baking stone, open the oven door and with a quick and confident jerk, slide the pizza from the peel onto the stone. Sometimes it's best to jiggle the pizza a little before you open the door, just to be sure it's not stuck to the peel. If you're using a baking sheet, on the other hand, simply place it in the top rack of the preheated oven, working quickly so the oven temperature doesn't drop too much. Bake until the crust is blistered and brown and the top is bubbling, about 5-7 minutes.

A TRUE NEAPOLITAN PIZZA is an exercise in restraint. You should be able to taste the wheatiness of the dough, the sweet acidity of the tomato sauce, and one or two other ingredients—max! Whatever you do, keep it simple and never, never use pizza as an excuse to clean out the refrigerator.

nancy harmon jenkins

Neapolitan Carnival Pie
Pizza Rustica alla Napoletana

MAKES ONE (9 INCH) (23 CM) PIE, ABOUT 8 SERVINGS

THIS MOST TYPICAL savory pie is served at Carnevale (the day before Ash Wednesday) and then again at Easter. Note that the dough is sweet—this is the traditional way of preparing it. If the combination is not appealing, leave out the sugar—but the dough may be slightly dry and need a bit of water to moisten it.

nick malgieri

1 recipe Pasta Frolla dough, medium batch (see page 151)

The Filling

1 pound (450 g) whole milk ricotta cheese
3 large eggs
½ teaspoon freshly ground black pepper
3 tablespoons grated pecorino Romano cheese
6 ounces (175 g) mozzarella cheese, coarsely grated
¼ pound (115 g) sweet dried sausage or salami, peeled and diced
¼ pound (115 g) prosciutto, shredded
¼ cup chopped fresh parsley

METHOD Set a rack in the lowest level of the oven and preheat to 350°F (180°C). For the filling, place the ricotta in a bowl and stir it smooth with a rubber spatula. Stir in the remaining filling ingredients in order.

To assemble the pie, unwrap the pasta frolla onto a floured surface and knead it until smooth and malleable. Divide it into 2 equal pieces. Butter a 9 inch (23 cm) glass pie pan. Roll 1 piece into a disk to line the pie pan. Fit the dough into the pan and trim it even with the edge of the pan. Scrape the filling into the lined pan.

Roll the remaining dough to a 9 inch (23 cm) square and use a serrated pizza wheel to cut it into 10 strips.

Place 5 strips on the filling about 1 inch (2.5 cm) apart, severing the dough at the edge of the pan. Place the second 5 strips at a 45 degree angle to the first ones and sever the ends. Bake the pie for about 45 minutes, or until the dough is baked through and the filling is firm. Cool on a rack.

Serve the pie at room temperature. Cut the pie in wedges for service. Cover and refrigerate leftovers.

Breadsticks from Piemonte
Grissini

SERVES 4 TO 6

⅔ cup warm tap water

2 teaspoons active dry yeast

2 cups unbleached all-purpose flour

1½ teaspoons salt

4 tablespoons lard or olive oil

Cornmeal, for the pans

METHOD For the dough, pour the water into a bowl and whisk in the yeast. Set aside. In another bowl, combine the flour, salt and lard and rub together between the palms of your hands until finely mixed together. Stir in the liquid with a rubber spatula and continue to stir until a soft dough forms.

Scrape the dough out onto a floured work surface and knead briefly until smooth. Place the dough in an oiled bowl and turn over so the top is oiled. Cover with plastic wrap and allow to rise until double in bulk, about an hour.

After the dough has risen, scrape it out onto a floured work surface and fold it over on itself repeatedly to deflate. Return the dough to the bowl, cover and refrigerate it for at least an hour, or up to overnight.

When you are ready to form the breadsticks, cover 2 or 3 baking sheets or jelly roll pans with cornmeal and remove the dough from the refrigerator. Cut the dough into 3 pieces and roll each into a 12 inch (30 cm) rope. Cut each rope into 1 inch (2.5 cm) pieces. Roll each piece of dough under the palms of your hands until it is a thin strip about 12 inches (30 cm) long. Place on one of the prepared pans. Repeat with the remaining pieces of dough.

Let the breadsticks rise for about an hour, or until they puff slightly.

About 20 minutes before you intend to bake the breadsticks, set racks in the upper and lower thirds of the oven and preheat to 350°F (180°C). Bake the breadsticks about 20 to 30 minutes, or until they are golden, dry and crisp. Cool on the pans.

Store the breadsticks in a tin or other airtight container—they keep indefinitely.

HINT When measuring flour, make sure you gently spoon the flour into a dry measure cup without shaking or tapping the cup, then level it off at the top with the back of a knife or the blade of a metal spatula.

LONG A SPECIALTY OF

Piemonte in Northern Italy, these breadsticks are quite versatile—they may be made with lard or oil. The traditional grissini of Piemonte are usually made with lard, but olive oil works just as well and provides and excellent flavor, too. Thanks to Jeffrey Steingarten, food critic of *Vogue* magazine, for sharing this recipe.

nick malgieri

Neapolitan Pizza Dough Turnovers
Calzoni Napoletani

MAKES TWO MEDIUM CALZONI

The Pizza Dough
1½ cups unbleached all-purpose flour
½ teaspoon salt
⅔ cup warm tap water
1 teaspoon active dry yeast
1 tablespoon olive oil

The Filling
½ pound (225 g) whole milk ricotta cheese
½ pound (225 g) fresh mozzarella cheese, diced or coarsely grated
¼ pound (115 g) sweet dried Italian sausage, or salami, skinned and thinly sliced
¼ cup chopped fresh parsley or basil
Freshly ground black pepper to taste

THOUGH THEY ARE REALLY just turnovers made from pizza dough, calzoni may have many different fillings. This one of ricotta and mozzarella with dried sausage is a typical one.

nick malgieri

METHOD   To make the dough, combine the flour and salt in a bowl and stir well to mix. Measure the water into another bowl and whisk in the yeast, then the oil. Stir the liquid into the dry ingredients with a rubber spatula and continue to stir until the mixture forms a firm dough.

Scrape the dough to a lightly floured work surface and knead it briefly until it is smooth, about 2 or 3 minutes. Place the dough in an oiled bowl and turn it over so that the top is oiled. Cover the bowl with plastic wrap and let the dough rise at room temperature for about an hour, or until it is double in bulk.

While the dough is rising prepare the filling: combine the ingredients in a large bowl and stir well to mix. Cover with plastic wrap and refrigerate until needed. When you are ready to bake the calzoni, set racks in the upper and lower thirds of the oven and preheat to 450°F (230°C). Cover 2 baking sheets or jelly roll pans with parchment or foil. To form the calzoni, scrape the risen dough to a floured work surface and press to deflate it without folding it over. Cut the dough into 2 pieces and roll each to a 10 inch (25 cm) circle. Place each on 1 of the prepared pans. Divide the filling between the 2 calzoni, placing it off center. Moisten the dough around the filling with water, using a pastry brush and fold the dough over to make a pastry the shape of a half-circle. Press the edges well and fold the dough over on itself at the edge to seal it closed. Use the point of a paring knife to make several slashes in the top to allow steam to escape.

Bake the calzoni until the dough is baked through and they are a deep golden color, about 20 minutes. Halfway through the baking, switch racks so that the one on the bottom rack is on the top and vice versa. Cool on the pans on racks for about 5 minutes, then serve.

HINT   If your oven gives strong bottom heat, bake the one on the bottom on a doubled pan (2 pans stacked together) for better insulation.

Neapolitan Pizza Dough Turnovers (Calzoni Napoletani)

CHAPTER SIX

Desserts

ITALIANS ARE SWEET on desserts. It seems that not one would ever miss an opportunity to enjoy a sumptuous delight from the hands of a pastry chef. In Sicily, people eat horn-shaped pastries filled with pastry cream for breakfast. A common mid-morning pick-me-up is a gelato and brioche sandwich.

Usually, the Italian home cook will prepare a simple fruit-based dessert or a pudding to complement lunch, the main meal of the day. For holidays and special occasions, however, whole days are spent in the preparation of prodigious quantities of traditional family recipes.

When we think of dessert, ingredients common to our kitchens come to mind: sugar, butter, cream, flour, cinnamon, coffee, chocolate, nuts, etc. In reality, these seemingly common ingredients represent the trade routes of four continents and more than five millennia of culinary history.

Sugar cane is a native product of sub-Saharan Africa. As early as the fourth century B.C., it was cultivated in North Africa and Persia. It wasn't until the ninth century that sugar was introduced into Sicily and the Iberian peninsula by Moorish invaders. In medieval Europe, sugar was an expensive, luxury item used more as a condiment than an ingredient, honey being the common sweetener.

As a footnote to history, some food historians have found a correlation between the expulsion of the Jews from the Spanish Empire in 1492 and the appearance of sweet pastry throughout the rest of Europe. These Spanish and Sicilian Jews, forced from their homes, carried sugar with them, introducing the art of pastry-making to Northern and Eastern Europe.

Coffee is another African product, native to Ethiopia. In the sixteenth century, Spain and Portugal established coffee plantations in Colombia and Brazil. It is not surprising that as the popularity of coffee grew in Europe, so did the writing of the long-form novel.

In the 1870s, an Italian gentleman named Gaggia invented the espresso machine. This process, passing steam under pressure through ground coffee in order to express its essential flavor, has captured the world.

The word "chocolate" is derived from the Aztec *xocolatl*, "bitter water." Europeans were the first to combine chocolate and sugar to create that magnificent triumph of culinary physics—tempered chocolate. Today, this product is available in a wide range of quality. Using the best, as suggested in these recipes, will make a difference in the flavor of your desserts.

Cinnamon, perhaps the oldest spice in recorded history is referenced in the Bible. Native to the Far East, Arab traders maintained an international cinnamon monopoly for centuries, and popularized a very interesting story concerning its cultivation.

According to these traders, cinnamon came from a rain forest deep within Southeast Asia. Filled with dangerous wild beasts and cannibals, the journey to this distant, wild land was perilous at best. In this rain forest, there lived a species of carnivorous birds. They built their nests of cinnamon so high in the verdant canopy, that it was impossible for a man to reach. The clever traders would throw large pieces of meat up into the nests for a period of months, waiting for the birds to grow fat. When the weight became more than the nests could bear, they came plummeting to the ground, and the traders would gather the cinnamon.

In reality, this story was a complete falsehood. Cinnamon is the inner bark of an evergreen tree native to the rain forests of Ceylon. There are no wild beasts, nor wild men, nor meat-eating birds whatsoever involved in its production. The Arab traders invented this story to hide the relative ease with which cinnamon is found and, therefore, protect their monopoly.

Fortunately, the Chefs of Cucina Amore are sharing all of their secrets for the exquisite desserts in this chapter.

Fallen Chocolate-Hazelnut Soufflé

THE COMBINATION OF

chocolate and hazelnut paste

is called *gianduja*. This is

a delicious flavor and I hope

you will have no problem

finding a good quality gian-

duja in your local specialty

food store. If you cannot

find any gianduja substitute

additional bittersweet

chocolate and hazelnuts.

joe simone

SERVES 10

¾ cup sugar, plus more for coating the pan
½ pound (225 g) bittersweet chocolate, preferably El Rey
½ pound (225 g) gianduja or milk chocolate, preferably Valhrona
½ pound (225 g) unsalted butter
2 ounces (60 g) espresso or strong coffee

1 teaspoon vanilla extract
6 eggs, separated
½ cup chopped toasted hazelnuts
Whipped cream, for garnish
Confectioners' sugar, for garnish
Chopped toasted hazelnuts, for garnish, optional

METHOD Several hours before serving or the night before, preheat the oven to 325°F (170°C). Spray a 10 inch (25 cm) springform pan with pan release and coat the inside of the pan with sugar.

Over a double boiler, melt the chocolates with the butter, espresso or strong coffee and vanilla.

While the chocolate is melting, place the egg yolks and half of the sugar in a clean mixing bowl. Whisk until the yolks are pale yellow and frothy to the ribbon stage, about 3 minutes at medium-high speed.

When the chocolate is melted, remove it from the heat and stir in the egg yolk mixture and the chopped hazelnuts. Set aside.

Clean the mixing bowl very well. Add the egg whites and whip with the remaining ½ cup sugar until it forms soft shiny peaks. Fold the whites into the chocolate mixture. Gently pour the batter into the prepared pan and bake in the preheated oven until a cake tester comes out "medium-rare," about 20-30 minutes. The cake will puff up a little and slightly crack on top. There should be a slight jiggle in the middle. Remove the pan from the oven and let cool to room temperature. This is a soufflé that will fall as it cools. Refrigerate it for several hours or overnight. You can also wrap it in two layers of plastic wrap and freeze it for up to one month.

Remove from the refrigerator just before serving. To serve, use a hot wet knife to cut into 10 pieces. Garnish with the whipped cream, confectioners' sugar and chopped toasted hazelnuts.

HINTS Be sure not to overcook the cake. It will puff up like any soufflé and then the top will begin to crack. At this point you should test the cake with a toothpick and if it comes out still a bit runny in the center—perfect! Do not be alarmed by the cake falling as it cools.

I keep one on hand in my feezer for unexpected guests.

Fallen Chocolate-Hazelnut Soufflé

Mocha Panna Cotta

SERVES 10

5 teaspoons gelatin powder, soaked in
    2 tablespoons cold water for 10 minutes
5 cups heavy whipping cream
1 cup espresso or very strong coffee
½ pound (225 g) bittersweet chocolate,
    broken up, preferably El Rey

1 tablespoon vanilla extract
7 ounces (200 g) sweetened condensed milk
Garnish of your choice: chocolate or caramel
    sauce, chopped nuts, fresh berries

METHOD   Add the cream and the espresso to a saucepan and bring to a simmer. Remove from the heat and stir in the chocolate and vanilla, stirring constantly until the chocolate melts and is fully mixed. The consistency will be thick. Add the condensed milk and the softened gelatin and stir until fully incorporated and the gelatin is fully melted. Pour into individual small custard cups and let sit in the refrigerator until set, about 6 hours or overnight.

To serve, run a thin knife around the edge of the custard cup and set in a pan of hot water. Invert onto serving plates and serve with the garnish of your choice.

PANNA COTTA LITERALLY means "cooked cream" in Italian. In this version, I have paired two of my favorite flavors: coffee and chocolate. The custard has a texture similar to crème brûlée but you do not bake it and there are no eggs in this recipe.

joe simone

Mocha Panna Cotta

Pan di Spagna

THIS "SPANISH BREAD"

is the most popular type of

cake in Italy. It is used as a

foundation for many elaborate

desserts, such as cassata and

zuppa inglese, and is even

often served unadorned to

accompany tea or coffee.

nick malgieri

MAKES ONE (10 INCH) (25 CM) CAKE

⅔ cup all-purpose flour
½ cup cornstarch
5 large eggs, separated

1 cup sugar
2 teaspoons vanilla extract
Pinch salt

METHOD   Set a rack in the middle level of the oven and preheat to 350°F (180°C). Butter a 9 or 10 inch (23 or 25 cm) springform pan and line the bottom with a disk of buttered parchment or wax paper

In a small bowl, stir together the flour and cornstarch and transfer the mixture to a sifter or strainer; set aside.

In the bowl of an electric mixer fitted with the whisk attachment, whip together the egg yolks, half the sugar and the vanilla on medium speed for 2 or 3 minutes, or until they are very light and fluffy.

In a clean, dry mixer bowl fitted with a clean dry whisk attachment, whip the egg whites and salt on medium speed until white and opaque. Whip the remaining sugar 1 tablespoon at a time, continuing to whip until the egg whites hold a firm peak. Using a large rubber spatula, fold the yolk mixture into the egg whites, then sift over and fold in the flour and starch mixture, in 3 or 4 additions. Scrape the batter into the prepared pan and smooth the top. Bake in the preheated oven until it is well risen, well colored and beginning to shrink away from the sides of the pan, about 30 to 40 minutes.

Run a knife around the side of the cake to loosen it from the pan and remove the springform side. Slide the cake, still on the paper to a rack to cool. Double wrap the cake layer in plastic and store it in the refrigerator for up to several days. Freeze for longer storage.

HINT   When folding the dry ingredients into the whipped eggs, dig down to the bottom of the bowl with your rubber spatula. Often lumps of flour get stuck in the bottom of the bowl and if you don't get them mixed into the batter, the baked cake will be riddled with little pellets of raw flour.

Mascarpone Sponge Cake Pudding
Tiramisù

MAKES A 2 QUART (2 L) SERVING DISH, ABOUT 10 TO 12 SERVINGS

1 recipe Pan di Spagna (see page 142)

The Espresso Syrup
1 cup strong brewed espresso
⅓ cup sugar
⅓ cup brandy or coffee-flavored liqueur

The Mascarpone Filling
4 large egg yolks
⅓ cup sugar
¼ cup sweet Marsala or other sweet wine
1 pound (450 g) mascarpone cheese,
    at room temperature
Cocoa powder or shaved semisweet
    chocolate, for finishing

METHOD   Bake and cool the pan di Spagna. Cut into thin vertical slices.

To make the espresso syrup, stir the sugar into the hot coffee to dissolve. Stir in the brandy.

To make the mascarpone filling, whisk the egg yolks, sugar and wine in the bowl of an electric mixer. Whisk the mixture over a pan of simmering water until it becomes foamy and thickened, about 2 or 3 minutes. Place on mixer with whisk attachment and whip on medium speed until cooled. Whip in the mascarpone.

To assemble, place a layer of the cake slices in the bottom of a 2 quart (2 l) gratin dish or other serving dish the dish and moisten them with a third of the syrup, using a brush. Spread with a third of the filling. Top with more cake slices, then another third of the syrup and another third of the filling. Finish with more cake, then the remaining syrup and filling. Shake cocoa or chocolate shavings over the top of the filling. Loosely cover with plastic wrap and refrigerate for several hours before serving.

Spoon the tiramisù out onto dessert plates or into dessert bowls. Cover and refrigerate leftovers.

THE NAME OF THIS DESSERT literally means "pick me up." Though it originated in Venice and Treviso, it is now popular all over Italy and all over the world. You may use pan di Spagna to make it, as we do here, or substitute bought lady fingers or imported Italian Savoiardi, a cookie very much like a crisp ladyfinger.

nick malgieri

THIS ELEGANT DESSERT

uses pan di Spagna to line a

bowl which is then filled with

a rich chocolate mousse. The

almonds and hazelnuts add a bit

of crunch to the rich filling.

nick malgieri

Chocolate-Filled Dome Cake
Zuccotto alla Cioccolata

MAKES A 1½ QUART (1.5 L) BOWL, ABOUT 8 TO 10 SERVINGS

1 recipe Pan di Spagna (see page 142)
1 pound (450 g) semisweet or bittersweet
  chocolate
1¼ cups heavy cream
½ cup toasted sliced almonds
½ cup toasted and skinned hazelnuts,
  crushed

4 egg whites
⅔ cup sugar
Italian brandy, for sprinkling the pan
  di Spagna
Confectioners' sugar and cocoa powder,
  for finishing

METHOD   Bake and cool the pan di Spagna. Cut into thin vertical slices.

To make the filling, cut the chocolate finely and place it in a mixing bowl. Bring the cream to a boil and pour over the chocolate. Let stand 2 minutes, then whisk smooth. Refrigerate, stirring often until cool, but not hard.

While the chocolate mixture is chilling, butter a 1½ quart (1.5 l) bowl and line with plastic wrap. Line the prepared bowl with the slices of pan di Spagna, overlapping them slightly. Sprinkle the cake with the brandy and cover loosely with plastic wrap.

When the chocolate filling has cooled, combine the egg whites and sugar in the bowl of an electric mixer and whisk over a pan of simmering water until the egg whites are hot and the sugar is dissolved. Place on mixer and whip on medium speed until cooled.

Place the cooled chocolate mixture on mixer and beat to lighten. Fold in the almonds and hazelnuts, then the meringue. Pour the filling into the prepared mold and cover with more slices of pan di Spagna. Cover with plastic wrap and refrigerate until set, several hours.

Invert a platter on the mold and invert the zuccotto on the platter. Remove the bowl and the plastic wrap. Sprinkle the zuccotto with the confectioners' sugar, then with a little of the cocoa powder.

Chocolate-Filled Dome Cake
(Zuccotto alla Cioccolata)

Arborio Rice Pudding with Currants and Dark Brown Sugar

THIS IS ONE OF THOSE "stick to your ribs" desserts. I love the texture that arborio rice gives you. The currants give a nice sweetness and flavor to the rice pudding— but you can substitute any other dried fruit.

joe simone

SERVES 4 TO 6

1½ cups arborio rice
1½ cups heavy whipping cream
1½ cups whole milk
2 cinnamon sticks
½ cup firmly packed dark brown sugar

½ cup firmly packed sultanas or
  golden raisins
½ cup firmly packed dried currants
  or dark raisins
Whipped cream, for garnish

METHOD   Place the rice, cream, milk and cinnamon sticks in a large saucepan set over medium heat. Bring to a gentle simmer and cook until the rice is tender, about 20-30 minutes. It is very important to keep the cream/milk mixture at a gentle simmer to avoid fast evaporation. The rice needs a chance to absorb all the milk.

Remove from the heat and stir in the sugar until all of the sugar dissolves. Stir in the sultanas or golden raisins and the currants or dark raisins. Let cool at least 15 minutes, stirring often. Before serving, remove the cinnamon sticks. Divide into individual serving bowls and top with a spoonful of the whipped cream. Serve immediately.

HINT   This recipe should not be made in advance. At the most, make it about 1 hour before serving and hold to keep warm in a hot water bath.

*Arborio Rice Pudding with Currants
and Dark Brown Sugar*

Sicilian Ricotta-Filled Easter Cake
Cassata alla Siciliana

THIS TRADITIONAL SICILIAN

Easter cake is made with *pan di Spagna*, or Spanish bread. Popular throughout southern Europe, pan di Spagna is used as a foundation for many types of cakes and desserts.

This Easter cake is a big production to prepare, but is well worth the trouble. For a simpler, but not traditional finish, spread the outside of the cake with sweetened whipped cream instead of the almond paste.

nick malgieri

MAKES ONE (10 INCH) (25 CM) CAKE, ABOUT 12 SERVINGS

1 recipe Pan di Spagna (see page 142)

The Ricotta Filling

3 pounds (1.4 kg) whole milk ricotta cheese, drained in a strainer lined with cheesecloth overnight in the refrigerator

2 cups confectioners' sugar

1 teaspoon vanilla extract

½ teaspoon cinnamon

4 ounces (115 g) semisweet chocolate, cut into ⅛ inch (3 mm) pieces

The Moistening Syrup

½ cup water

½ cup sugar

1 teaspoon vanilla extract

The Pasta Reale

7-8 ounces (200-225 g) almond paste

2 cups confectioners' sugar

3-4 tablespoons light corn syrup

Green food coloring

Cornstarch, for rolling

For Decoration

1 egg white

1½ cups confectioners' sugar

¼ teaspoon lemon juice or white vinegar

Candied citron

Candied cherries

METHOD   Bake and cool the pan di Spagna.

To make the filling, place the ricotta in a mixing bowl and gently stir in the confectioners' sugar with a rubber spatula to avoid making the filling too liquid. Remove ½ cup of the filling to spread on the outside of the cake later on; cover and refrigerate. Stir the remaining ingredients into the rest of the filling; cover and refrigerate until needed.

For the syrup, bring the sugar and water to a boil in a small saucepan over low heat, stirring occasionally. Cool and stir in the vanilla.

To assemble the cassata, butter and line a 10 inch (25 cm) pie pan with plastic wrap. Cut out a 12 inch (30 cm) cardboard or set aside a flat platter for unmolding the cake.

Use a sharp serrated knife to cut the pan di Spagna into thin vertical slices. Line the prepared pan, bottom and sides, with the slices of cake and sprinkle with about a quarter of the syrup. Spread half the ricotta filling in the bottom of the pan. Cover the filling with a layer of cake slices and moisten the cake with more syrup, using a brush. Spread the remaining filling on the cake and cover with another layer of the cake slices. Sprinkle sparingly with the syrup (this will be the bottom of the cake and you need to avoid having it too wet). Wrap and refrigerate the cassata for several hours or overnight. Reserve and refrigerate the remaining syrup for the outside of the cake.

While the cassata is chilling, make the pasta reale: combine the almond paste and confectioners' sugar in the work bowl of a food processor fitted with the steel blade. Pulse repeatedly until the mixture resembles fine crumbs. Add the corn syrup and pulse until the dough forms a ball. Scrape the pasta reale to the work surface and add the food coloring. Knead in the color to tint the pasta reale a pale green. Wrap in plastic and reserve at room temperature until needed.

For the icing, place the egg white and sugar in the bowl of an electric mixer fitted with the whisk attachment. Whip on medium speed until mixed. Add the lemon juice and continue mixing until light and fluffy, about 5 minutes. Press plastic wrap against the surface of the icing and reserve until needed.

To finish the cassata, unwrap it and invert the cardboard or platter onto the top of the cake. Invert and remove the pie pan. Paint the outside of the cassata with the remaining syrup and spread it with the reserved filling, using a small metal offset spatula. Set aside.

Dust the work surface with cornstarch and unwrap the pasta reale onto it. Roll the paste thinly and use it to cover the cassata. Trim the excess even with the base of the cake.

Fit a pastry bag with a small plain tube and decorate the outside of the cassata with the icing. Accent with the candied fruit.

Keep the cassata in a cool place until ready to serve it. Wrap and refrigerate leftovers.

Two Color Trifle
Zuppa a Due Colori

THIS ITALIAN VERSION

of an English trifle uses two
different flavored (and colored) pastry creams alternat-
ed with slices of liqueur
syrup-soaked pan di Spagna.

nick malgieri

MAKES A 2 QUART (2 L) BOWL, ABOUT 12 SERVINGS

1 recipe Pan di Spagna (see page 142)

The Pastry Creams

1 quart (1 l) milk

1¼ cups sugar

10 egg yolks

¾ cup all-purpose flour

2 tablespoons orange liqueur

2 teaspoons vanilla extract

1 teaspoon cinnamon

6 ounces (175 g) bittersweet chocolate
  melted with ½ cup milk

The Syrup

1 cup water

1 cup sugar

⅓ cup dark rum

¼ cup Strega or other herb liqueur

Chocolate shavings, for finishing

METHOD   Bake and cool the pan di Spagna. Cut into thin vertical slices.

To make the pastry creams, bring the milk and half the sugar to a boil in a large saucepan. Whisk the egg yolks in a mixing bowl and whisk in the remaining sugar. Sift in the flour and whisk it in. Whisk a third of the boiling milk into the egg mixture. Return the remaining milk to a boil and whisk in the egg mixture, continuing to whisk, especially in the corners of the pan, until the pastry cream thickens and comes to a boil. Cook, whisking about 1 minute.

Divide the pastry cream between 2 bowls, placing an equal amount in each. To the first bowl, stir in the orange liqueur and vanilla extract. To the second bowl, add the chocolate and milk mixture and the cinnamon and stir them in. Press plastic wrap against the surface of the cream in each bowl and refrigerate until cold, several hours, or overnight.

For the syrup, bring the water and sugar to a boil in a saucepan over medium heat, stirring occasionally. Cool and stir in the rum and the liqueur.

To assemble the zuppa, place a layer of the cake slices in the bottom of a 2½-3 quart (2.5-3 l) trifle bowl or other glass bowl and moisten them with the syrup using a brush. Spread on a third of the chocolate cream. Top with a layer of cake slices and more syrup and half the orange cream. Cover the orange cream with more cake and syrup and another third of the chocolate cream. Top with more cake and syrup and the remaining orange cream. Lastly, top with cake, syrup and the remaining choco-late cream. Sprinkle the chocolate cream with the chocolate shavings and cover with plastic wrap. Refrigerate until ready to serve. To serve, spoon the zuppa out onto dessert plates or into dessert bowls.

HINT   A zuppa may be prepared up to a day in advance. Cover tightly with plastic wrap and refrigerate. Sprinkle with the chocolate shavings just before serving.

Pasta Frolla
Italian Sweet Pastry Dough

Large Recipe

3 cups all-purpose flour

½ cup sugar

1 teaspoon baking powder

¾ teaspoon salt

12 tablespoons (1½ sticks) unsalted butter
   or lard

3 large eggs

Medium Recipe

2 cups all-purpose flour

⅓ cup sugar

¾ teaspoon baking powder

½ teaspoon salt

8 tablespoons (1 stick) unsalted butter
   or lard

2 large eggs

METHOD   To make the dough in the food processor, place the dry ingredients in a work bowl fitted with the steel blade. Pulse several times to mix. Add the butter and pulse 8 or 10 times, to mix in. Then add the eggs and continue to pulse until the dough forms a ball.

To mix the dough by hand, place the dry ingredients in a large bowl and stir well to mix. Add the butter and rub the mixture between the palms of your hands until it forms fine crumbs. Add the eggs and stir in with a fork, continuing to stir until the dough leaves the sides of the bowl. Form the dough into a ball.

Wrap the dough in plastic and chill until needed, up to several days.

When ready to use the dough, unwrap and place it on a floured work surface. Knead the dough until it is soft and malleable.

HINT   Try to leave enough time so you can chill the dough for an hour before you try to roll it. But, before rolling the dough, knead it lightly on a floured work surface to make it malleable — it will roll out more easily.

THIS IS A TYPICAL RECIPE for the multi-purpose Italian sweet pastry dough. It is easy to make in the food processor, but may also be made by hand.

Frolla means friable, not a word that most Americans use every day: it signifies crumbly — cookie like — and that is exactly the texture that a good pasta frolla should have. A far cry from our typical flaky pie dough, pasta frolla is used almost universally for making pies and tarts in Italy. It is even used sometimes with a savory filling, as in the case of a pizza rustica.

nick malgieri

Caramelized Walnut Tart from Val d'Aosta
Torta Valdostana

THIS WONDERFUL WALNUT pastry is popular in Aosta, capital city of the Valle d'Aosta, in northwestern Italy. Near the French border, the region is famous for its butter and walnuts.

nick malgieri

MAKES ONE (10 INCH) (25 CM) TART, ABOUT 12 SERVINGS

The Walnut Filling
½ cup sugar
½ teaspoon lemon juice
½ cup honey
4 tablespoons (½ stick) unsalted butter, cut into 8 pieces
Pinch salt
2½ cups chopped walnuts

The Pasta Frolla Dough
16 tablespoons (2 sticks) unsalted butter, softened
1 cup sugar
4 large egg yolks
1 teaspoon vanilla extract
2¾ cups all-purpose flour
Confectioners' sugar, for dusting

METHOD   To make the walnut filling, combine the sugar and lemon juice in a medium saucepan and stir well to mix. Place over medium heat and stir occasionally until the sugar melts and caramelizes. When the sugar is a medium amber-caramel color, add the honey and butter so that the sugar ceases darkening. Swirl the pan to mix them in and allow the mixture to return to a boil. Boil hard for a minute, remove from the heat and stir in the salt and walnuts. Pour the mixture into a buttered bowl and set aside to cool.

Set a rack in the lowest level of the oven and preheat to 350°F (180°C).

Butter a 10 inch (25 cm) round pan, 2 inches (5 cm) deep and line the bottom with a disk of buttered parchment or wax paper.

For the pasta frolla dough, beat together the butter and sugar in the bowl of an electric mixer fitted with the paddle attachment on medium speed until soft and very light, about 5 minutes. Beat in the egg yolks one at a time, beating smooth after each addition. Beat in the vanilla. Remove the bowl from the mixer and use a large rubber spatula to stir in the flour until the mixture forms a very soft dough. Scrape a little more than half the dough into the prepared pan and use the floured palm of your hand to press the dough evenly in the bottom of the pan. Use fingertips to press the dough about halfway up the side of the pan. Scrape in the filling.

To form the top crust, flour a cardboard disk the same diameter as the pan and press the dough out onto it. Use a long spatula or knife to scrape the dough from the cardboard, sliding it over the filling in the pan. Use the back of a spoon to smooth the dough into place. Pierce the top crust every inch (2.5 cm) or so with a fork. Bake until the dough is firm and golden, about 45 minutes. Cool in the pan on a rack.

To unmold, invert the tart onto a flat plate or cutting board. Remove the pan and paper and replace with a platter. Invert again and remove the top plate. Dust lightly with the confectioners' sugar. Keep leftovers covered at room temperature.

HINT   For advance preparation, wrap and freeze, but bring to room temperature before serving.

Caramelized Walnut Tart from Val d'Aosta (Torta Valdostana)

No-Bake Ricotta Tart

FRESH RICOTTA TOPS

a pastry shell and is covered with fresh berries — what could be easier? Use Nick Malgieri's recipe for *Pasta Frolla* (see page 151), or make a cookie-crumb crust. In Italy, it would be made with sheep's milk.

faith willinger

SERVES 8

2 cups whole milk ricotta cheese
1-2 tablespoons granulated sugar
1 tablespoon honey
1 teaspoon grated lemon zest

1 pint (500 ml) berries, such as strawberries, raspberries, or blueberries
1 (9 inch) (23 cm) pastry/pie shell, pre-baked

METHOD   In a food processor or blender or with an immersion mixer, beat the ricotta, sugar, honey and lemon zest until smooth. Clean and slice the strawberries. If you are using other berries, clean and pick them over. Fill the pastry shell with the ricotta cheese mixture and top with the fruit. Serve immediately.

No-Bake Ricotta Tart

Tartlets Filled with Rice and Ricotta Cream
Tortelli di Riso

THESE RICE TARTLETS

are usually made in deep oval

molds in Italy. Here, we would

substitute muffin pans or

individual tartlet pans with

removable bottoms.

nick malgieri

MAKES 18 TARTS, DEPENDING ON THE SIZE MOLDS USED

1 recipe Pasta Frolla, medium recipe
  (see page 151)

The Rice Filling

⅓ cup arborio rice

¼ teaspoon salt

3 tablespoons butter

⅓ cup sugar

2¼ cups milk

1 cup ricotta cheese

3 large eggs

1 teaspoon finely grated lemon zest

1 teaspoon vanilla extract

½ cup raisins, optional

METHOD   Prepare and chill the pasta frolla dough.

To make the rice filling, bring a large pan of water to a boil and add the rice and salt. Stir well to prevent the rice from sticking and return to a boil. Lower to a simmer and cook the rice until it's very tender, about 15 minutes. Drain the rice.

Combine the cooked rice, butter, sugar, and milk in a large saucepan and bring to a boil, stirring often, over medium heat. Lower to a simmer and cook until thick and creamy, about 20 minutes. Cool the rice mixture.

In a large bowl stir the ricotta smooth with a rubber spatula. Stir in the eggs, one at a time, then stir in the zest and vanilla. Stir in the rice mixture smoothly.

Set a rack in the lowest level of the oven and preheat to 350°F (180°C).

Butter two 12-cavity muffin pans. Divide the pasta frolla dough into 18 pieces, roll each to a circle and line one of the muffin pan cavities with it. Trim the dough even with the top of the pan. Fill each about two thirds full with the rice filling, then fold the excess dough over onto the filling all around. Bake the tortelli about 30 minutes, or until the dough is baked through and the filling is firm. Cool in the pan on a rack. Place another rack on the muffin pan and invert to unmold the tortelli. Stand them right-side-up on a platter.

Serve the tortelli at room temperature. Wrap and refrigerate leftovers.

HINT   For an interesting variation, add ½ cup plump golden or dark raisins to the filling after everything else is in.

Tartlets Filled with Rice and Ricotta Cream (Tortelli di Riso)

Roman Lattice-Topped Apple Tart
Crostata di Mele alla Romana

MAKES ONE (12 INCH) (30 CM) TART, ABOUT 10 SERVINGS

1 recipe Pasta Frolla, large recipe
(see page 151)

The Apple Filling
3 pounds (1.4 kg) Golden Delicious apples
½ cup sugar

2 tablespoons butter
2 tablespoons dark rum
½ teaspoon ground cinnamon
1 egg well beaten with a pinch of salt
(egg wash)

METHOD   Prepare and chill the pasta frolla dough.

For the apple filling, peel, core and slice the apples thinly. Combine with the remaining ingredients and place in a saucepan over low heat. Cover the pan and cook for 10 minutes, until the apples have exuded their juices. Uncover and continue cooking until the filling is fairly dry. Remove from the heat and let cool.

Set a rack in the lower third and preheat the oven to 350°F (180°C). Cover a cookie sheet or jelly roll pan with parchment or foil.

Unwrap and knead the pasta frolla dough until smooth on a floured surface. Roll half the dough to a 12 inch (30 cm) disk and transfer to the prepared pan. Cut to a perfect 12 inch (30 cm) circle using a plate or other pattern. Spread the cooled filling to within ½ inch (1.5 cm) of the edge of the dough. Roll two thirds of the remaining dough to a rectangle and cut into narrow strips. Brush the strips with the egg wash and arrange on the filling in a diagonal lattice. Use the scraps and remaining dough to make a long cylinder. Brush the edge of the tart and apple cylinder with the remaining egg wash. Make diagonal impressions in the cylinder with the back of a knife. Bake the tart until the dough is baked through and nicely colored, about 30 minutes. Cool the tart on the pan.

Pastry Cream and Sour Cherry Pie
Pizza di Crema e Amarene

MAKES ONE (9 INCH) (23 CM) PIE, ABOUT 8 SERVINGS

1 recipe Pasta Frolla, medium recipe
(see page 151)

The Pastry Cream Filling

2 cups milk

⅔ cup sugar, divided

5 egg yolks

½ cup all-purpose flour

1 teaspoon finely grated lemon zest

1 teaspoon finely grated orange zest

2 teaspoons vanilla extract

½ cup sour cherry jam

Confectioners' sugar, for dusting

THIS PIE OF CITRUS-scented pastry cream and sour cherry jam is a Neapolitan favorite. In season, strawberries sometimes replace the jam.

nick malgieri

METHOD   Prepare and chill the pasta frolla dough.

To make the pastry cream, bring the milk and half the sugar to a boil in a large saucepan. Whisk the egg yolks in a mixing bowl and whisk in the remaining sugar. Sift in the flour and whisk it in.

Whisk ⅓ of the boiling milk into the egg mixture. Return the remaining milk to a boil and whisk in the egg mixture, continuing to whisk, especially in the corners, until the pastry cream thickens and comes to a boil. Cook, whisking, about 1 minute. Off heat, whisk in the zests and vanilla. Scrape the pastry cream into a shallow glass or stainless steel pan and press plastic wrap against the surface. Chill at least 1 hour.

Set a rack in the lowest level of the oven and preheat to 350°F (180°C). Butter a 9 inch (23 cm) glass pie pan.

To assemble the pie, unwrap the pasta frolla onto a floured surface and knead it until smooth and malleable. Divide it into 2 equal pieces. Roll 1 piece into a disk to line the pie pan. Fit the dough into the pan and trim it even with the edge of the pan. Scrape half the pastry cream into the lined pan. Stir the jam to liquefy it and spoon as even a layer as possible on the pastry cream. Spoon over the other half of the pastry cream. Roll the remaining dough to a 10 inch (25 cm) circle and center it on the filling. Tuck the edge of the top crust under the edge of the bottom crust. Do not flute the edge of the pie. Pierce several vent holes in the top of the pie with the point of a paring knife. Bake the pie until the dough is baked through and a deep golden color, about 45 minutes. If the filling shows signs of simmering, remove the pie from the oven. Cool the pie on a rack, then chill it for several hours to set the filling.

Sprinkle with the confectioners' sugar before serving. Cut the pie in wedges for service. Cover and refrigerate leftovers.

HINT   To make *Pizza di Crema Cioccolata*, omit the lemon and orange zests from the pastry cream. In their place, add 4 ounces (115 g) semisweet chocolate, cut into ¼ inch (6 mm) pieces, and ¼ teaspoon ground cinnamon to the pastry cream along with the vanilla, whisking it in until smooth. Then stir in ¼ cup citron, cut into ¼ inch (6 mm) dice. Omit the sour cherry jam.

Neapolitan Wheat Berry and Ricotta Pie
Pastiera di Grano

Neapolitan pastry. A ricotta filling studded with cooked wheat berries in encased in a sweet crust. It is the wheat pie or grain pie served at Easter that so many Italian Americans remember their grandmothers preparing. Seen in all the pastry shops in Naples, it is also very popular in Rome and throughout Southern Italy.

nick malgieri

MAKES ONE (9 INCH) (23 CM) PIE, ABOUT 8 SERVINGS

1 recipe Pasta Frolla, medium recipe
  (see page 151)
½ cup hulled (white) wheat kernels,
  if unavailable, substitute rice
½ teaspoon salt

The Ricotta Filling

1 pound (450 g) whole milk ricotta cheese
⅓ cup sugar

2 large eggs
1 teaspoon grated orange zest
1 teaspoon vanilla extract
1 teaspoon orange flower water, optional
¼ cup diced candied orange peel
Cinnamon, for finishing

METHOD Prepare and chill the pasta frolla dough.

Place the wheat kernels and salt in a 4 quart (3.75 l) saucepan and add 2 quarts (2 l) of water. Bring to a boil over medium heat, then lower to a simmer. Cook until the wheat is tender—up to 2 hours, adding water as necessary to keep them from drying out and scorching. When the wheat is cooked, drain in a strainer and rinse it under running cold water. Reserve covered and refrigerated until ready to make the filling.

Set a rack in the lowest level of the oven and preheat to 350°F (180°C).

To make the filling, stir the ricotta and sugar together in a large bowl. Stir in the eggs, one at a time, then stir in the flavorings. Stir in the cooled wheat kernels. To assemble the pie, butter a 9 inch (23 cm) glass pie pan. Unwrap the pasta frolla onto a floured surface and knead it until smooth and malleable. Divide it into 2 equal pieces. Roll 1 piece into a disk to line the prepared pie pan. Fit the dough into the pan and trim it even with the edge of the pan. Scrape the filling into the lined pan and sprinkle it with cinnamon, if you wish.

Roll the remaining dough to a 9 inch (23 cm) square and use a serrated pizza wheel to cut it into 10 strips. Place 5 strips on the filling about 1 inch (2.5 cm) apart, severing the dough at the edge of the pan. Place the second 5 strips at a 45 degree angle to the first ones and sever the ends. Bake the pastiera until the dough is baked through and the filling is firm, about 45 minutes. Cool on a rack.

Serve the pastiera at room temperature, cut into wedges for service. Cover and refrigerate leftovers.

Neapolitan Wheat Berry and Ricotta Pie
(Pastiera di Grano)

Capri Cake
Torta Caprese

THOUGH CHOCOLATE CAKES

are not a usual part of the Italian

dessert repertoire, this one

is seen in all the elegant pastry

shops in Naples.

nick malgieri

MAKES ONE (10 INCH) (25 CM) CAKE, ABOUT 12 SERVINGS

1½ sticks (12 tablespoons) unsalted butter, softened	8 large eggs, separated
¾ cup sugar	1½ cups (about 5-6 ounces (150-175 g) ground almonds
7 ounces (200 g) semisweet chocolate, melted and cooled	¾ cup all-purpose flour
	Confectioners' sugar, for finishing

METHOD   Set a rack in the middle level of the oven and preheat to 350°F (180°C). Butter a 10 inch (25 cm) round cake pan, 2 inches (5 cm) deep and line with a disk of parchment or wax paper.

In the bowl of an electric mixer fitted with the paddle attachment, beat together the butter and ¼ cup of the sugar until soft and light, about 2 or 3 minutes. Stop the mixer and add the chocolate, beating again until the mixture is smooth. Beat in the egg yolks, one at a time, beating smooth after each addition. Turn the mixer off and use a large rubber spatula to stir in the almonds and flour.

Pour the egg whites into a clean, dry mixer bowl and whip them by machine with the whisk attachment on medium speed until they are white and opaque and beginning to hold their shape.

Whip in the remaining sugar about a tablespoon at a time, continuing to whip the egg whites until they hold a soft, glossy peak. Stir about a quarter of the egg whites into the batter to lighten it, then use a large rubber spatula to fold in the remaining egg whites.

Scrape the batter into the prepared pan and smooth the top. Bake the cake until it is firm, about 35-40 minutes. If you use a toothpick or the point of a knife, insert it about 2 inches (5 cm) from the center of the cake and it should emerge dry.

Invert the cake to a rack and remove the pan. Immediately re-invert to another rack so that the cake cools right-side-up. If the cake sinks slightly in the center as it cools, trim away the sides before inverting the cake to a platter.

Dust the cake with the confectioners' sugar before serving.

HINT   Make sure cake pans are evenly buttered with soft, not melted, butter. This gives a thicker coating and makes it easier to unmold baked cakes.

"Delight" Cake
Torta Delizia

MAKES ONE 9 OR 10 INCH (23 OR 25 CM) CAKE, ABOUT 10 SERVINGS

1 recipe Pan di Spagna
(see page 142)

The Syrup
½ cup water
¼ cup sugar
1¼ cup white rum

The Topping
1½ pounds (750 g) almond paste, cut into
1 inch (2.5 cm) pieces
4 large eggs
2 tablespoons white rum

The Filling
½-¾ cup sour cherry or other jam
Confectioners' sugar, for finishing

THIS IS A CLASSIC FOUND in pastry shops throughout Italy in varying versions. Although this cake is sometimes very sweet, the sugar has been kept to a minimum in this version so that both the flavor of the cake and the perfume of the almonds emerge.

nick malgieri

METHOD   Bake and cool the pan di Spagna.

For the syrup, bring the sugar and water to a boil in a small pan over medium heat stirring occasionally. Cool and add the rum.

For the topping, beat together the almond paste and one of the eggs in the bowl of an electric mixer fitted with the paddle attachment on medium speed, until softened. Add the remaining eggs, one at a time, beating smooth after each addition. Beat in the rum.

Set a rack in the middle level and preheat the oven to 400°F (200°C).

To assemble the cake, cut the cake in half horizontally and place half on a 10 inch (25 cm) piece of cardboard. Moisten the layer with half the syrup and spread with the jam. Top with the other cake layer and moisten with the remaining syrup. Spread the outside smoothly with the almond paste mixture using a metal icing spatula.

Fit a pastry bag with a ⅜ inch (9 mm) star tube or ribbon tube and half fill the bag with the remaining almond mixture. Pipe a series of vertical lines up the side of the cake, refilling the bag as necessary. Pipe straight lines to cover the entire top of the cake. Dust the outside of the cake lightly with the confectioners' sugar. Place the cake on a cookie sheet or the back of a jelly roll pan. Bake the cake until the outside is light golden, about 10-15 minutes. Cool on a rack.

Siena Fruitcake
Panforte di Siena

THIS MEDIEVAL FRUITCAKE

is the ancestor of our modern

ones. Sweet and chewy, panforte

is best enjoyed in small wedges

with coffee or sweet wine.

nick malgieri

MAKES ONE 8 INCH (20 CM) CAKE, ABOUT 20 SMALL SERVINGS

⅔ cup honey

⅔ cup sugar

⅔ cup finely diced citron or candied
  lemon peel

⅔ cup finely diced candied orange peel

1½ cups blanched almonds, lightly toasted
  and coarsely chopped

⅔ cup all-purpose flour

1 teaspoon cinnamon

½ teaspoon coriander

½ teaspoon cloves

½ teaspoon nutmeg

Flour, for dusting

Confectioners' sugar, for dusting

METHOD   Set a rack in the middle level of the oven and preheat to 300°F (150°C). Line the bottom and sides of a 8 inch (20 cm) diameter pan 2 inches (5 cm) deep, with buttered foil.

Combine the honey and sugar in a medium saucepan. Stir well to mix, then place on low heat. Cook, stirring occasionally, until the mixture comes to a full boil, then remove from heat.

Stir in the candied fruit and almonds. Stir together the flour and spices, add them to the batter, then stir until smooth.

Scrape the batter into the prepared pan and smooth the top. Sift a couple of tablespoons of the flour into the top of the panforte so it doesn't crust while baking — this will be removed later. Bake until the panforte is firm and gently simmering just around the edges, about 20-25 minutes. Cool in the pan on a rack.

When the panforte is completely cool, invert it to remove the flour from the top — use a dry brush to get it all off. Carefully peel away the foil and stand the panforte right-side-up. Wrap in plastic or foil and keep at room temperature — it keeps almost indefinitely.

To serve, sift a thin layer of the confectioners' sugar over the top. Serve small wedges — they are eaten out of hand, not with a fork.

Siena Fruitcake (Panforte di Siena)

Olive Oil Breakfast Cake

SERVES 6 TO 8

2 cups unbleached all-purpose flour
½ teaspoon baking powder
½ teaspoon baking soda
½ teaspoon vanilla extract
1¼ cups extra-virgin olive oil

1¼ cups whole milk
Zest of 3 oranges, grated
 (about 4 tablespoons)
3 eggs
1 cup sugar

IN ITALY, THIS LIGHTLY sweetened cake, aromatic with orange zest, is often served at breakfast but it could just as easily be a tea cake or dessert.

nancy harmon jenkins

METHOD   Butter and flour a 9 x 2 inch (23 x 5 cm) round cake pan. Preheat the oven to 350°F (180°C).

In a medium bowl, toss together the flour, baking powder and baking soda.

In another medium bowl or large measuring cup with a pouring lip, beat together the olive oil, milk and grated orange zest.

In another large bowl, beat the eggs, gradually incorporating the sugar, until the mixture is very thick and lemony colored. Beat in the vanilla. Gently fold in about one third of the flour into the egg mixture, using a rubber spatula. Fold in one third of the oil-milk combination. Continue mixing by thirds until all the flour and all the oil mixtures have been incorporated.

Pour the batter into the prepared pan and bake in the preheated oven until the cake is golden brown and springs away from the side of the pan, about 40-50 minutes.

Olive Oil Breakfast Cake

Greek Semolina-Yogurt Cake
with Hot Lemon Syrup

THIS SIMPLE BUT

delicious cake is based on an
old-fashioned Greek recipe.
The trick is pouring the hot
lemon syrup onto the hot
cake — the combination is
much, much greater than its
parts. It is lovely to look at,
and to eat, served with a
sauce of fresh strawberries
or raspberries, quickly
whizzed in the blender or
food processor with just
enough sugar to bring out
the flavors of the fruit.

nancy harmon jenkins

SERVES 10 TO 12

The Semolina-Yogurt Cake	**The Hot Lemon Syrup**
2 cups semolina flour	2 cups sugar
1⅔ cups sugar	1½ cups water
Zest of 1 lemon, grated	Juice of ½ lemon
1½ teaspoons baking powder	
2 cups plain low fat or nonfat yogurt	
⅓ cup light olive oil	

METHOD   For the semolina-yogurt cake, spray the bottom and sides of a 9 x 13 inch (23 x 33 cm) pan or an 11 inch (28 cm) springform pan with olive oil, or dip a paper towel in a little oil and rub it liberally over the bottom and sides of the pan. Preheat the oven to 350°F (180°C).

In a large bowl, mix the flour, sugar, lemon zest and baking powder, tossing with a fork to mix well. Add the yogurt and mix with a wooden spoon or spatula — do not use an electric mixer or an egg beater — just until everything is well combined. Stir in the olive oil and mix well. Pour the batter into the prepared pan. With a table knife, cut about ½ inch (1.5 cm) into the batter, making 10-12 diamond shapes or squares. The marks will not remain completely visible before baking, but when removed from the oven, the cake will be scored. Bake in the preheated oven until the cake is golden, about 40-45 minutes.

While the cake is baking, make the hot lemon syrup. In a small saucepan, bring the sugar, water and lemon juice to a boil. Simmer until it becomes a fairly thick syrup and reaches 215°F (100°C) on a candy thermometer, about 20-25 minutes. Set aside.

Remove the cake from the oven and cut through the scored portions, constantly cleaning the knife as you do so. Without removing the cake from the pan, pour over the hot syrup, tilting the pan slightly so that the syrup runs into all the crevices. It may seem like an excessive amount of syrup, but it soaks in well. Serve directly from the pan, on its own or with the strawberry or raspberry sauce mentioned above. Do not cover this cake until it is fully cooled off or it will become soggy and the lemon flavor will be overwhelming.

INGREDIENTS TIPS   Semolina flour, made from hard durum wheat, can be found in most well stocked supermarkets.

When grating lemon or orange zest, I like to use organically raised fruit, if at all possible, to minimize the contact with pesticides.

Greek Semolina-Yogurt Cake with Hot Lemon Syrup

Tuscan Apple Yogurt Cake

traditional ingredient in Tuscany—not at all! But it has been taken up by traditional cooks like Marta Goretti, who makes this moist, dense apple cake at her restaurant in the Casentino valley between Arezzo and Florence.

nancy harmon jenkins

SERVES 6 TO 8

⅔ cup yogurt
3 eggs
¼ cup extra-virgin olive oil
⅓ cup milk
1 teaspoon vanilla extract
2 cups unbleached all-purpose flour

⅔ cup sugar
Pinch sea salt
Pinch freshly grated nutmeg
1 teaspoon baking powder
2 tart apples, peeled and sliced
   very thinly

METHOD   Butter and flour a 9 x 2 inch (23 x 5 cm) round cake pan. Preheat the oven to 350°F (180°C).

In a large bowl, beat the yogurt, eggs, oil and milk until well mixed. Beat in the vanilla.

In a medium bowl, sift together the flour, sugar, salt, nutmeg and baking powder. Sift the dry ingredients over the liquid ingredients, adding about one third at a time, and gently folding in the dry ingredients with a spatula. Fold in the apple slices.

Spoon into the prepared pans and bake in the preheated oven until it browns on top, about 40-50 minutes. Let cool on a cake rack before turning out.

Venetian Carnival Pastries
Galani

MAKES ABOUT 30 PASTRIES

2½ cups unbleached all-purpose flour

3 tablespoons sugar

½ teaspoon salt

3 tablespoons butter or oil

3 large eggs

4 cups vegetable oil, for frying

METHOD To make the dough, place the flour in a large bowl and stir in the sugar and salt. Add the butter or oil and rub in, rubbing the mixture between the palms of your hands to mix it in finely. Add the eggs and stir them in with a fork, continuing to stir until the dough comes away from the sides of the bowl.

Scrape the dough out onto a floured work surface and knead it lightly, folding it over on itself repeatedly, until smooth, about 2 minutes, adding a tablespoon or 2 of flour if the dough is very sticky. Wrap and chill the dough for an hour.

Cover 2 baking sheets or jelly roll pans with parchment or foil to hold the galani before frying and cover 2 more pans with paper towels for draining them after frying.

Remove the dough from the refrigerator and unwrap it onto a floured work surface. Divide the dough into 4 pieces. Roll each piece to a 6 inch (15 cm) square, then cut the dough into 1½ inch (4 cm) strips. Cut across every 3 inches (8 cm) to make 1½ x 3 inch (4 x 8 cm) rectangles. Make a slash in the center of each rectangle and thread one of the ends through the slash. Place the galani on the prepared pans as they are formed. Repeat with the remaining pieces of dough.

When you are ready to fry the galani, place the oil in a large saucepan or Dutch oven. Heat the oil to 350°F (180°C) on medium heat. Fry the pastries a few at a time, stirring them to make sure they color evenly. Drain on the pans covered with paper towels.

Cool the galani and dust them with confectioners' sugar immediately before serving. These are best on the day they are made. Cover leftovers loosely with plastic wrap and store at room temperature.

THIS IS A TYPICAL

Carnival pastry of Venice. The tradition of fried pastries is strongly allied to Carnival throughout Europe, because most of the frying was done in animal fat — prohibited during the fast days of Lent which follow Carnival feasting.

nick malgieri

Sicilian Fried Tubes with Ricotta Filling
Cannoli alla Siciliana

MAKES ABOUT 12-18 SHELLS

The Cannoli Shells

2 cups all-purpose flour

1 tablespoon sugar

½ teaspoon salt

1 teaspoon cinnamon

4 tablespoons olive oil or lard

¼ cup white wine

¼ cup water

1 egg white, lightly beaten, to seal the shells

3 cups vegetable oil, for frying

The Ricotta Filling

2 pounds (900 g) whole milk ricotta cheese, drained in a strainer lined with cheesecloth overnight in the refrigerator

1½ cups confectioners' sugar

1 teaspoon vanilla extract

1 teaspoon white rum

1 ounce (30 g) chopped semisweet chocolate

Chopped pistachios, for garnish

Confectioners' sugar, for dusting

METHOD   To make the dough for the cannoli shells, pulse together the dry ingredients in the work bowl of a food processor fitted with the steel blade. Add the oil or lard and pulse again about half a dozen times to mix. Then add the wine and water and pulse again until the dough forms a ball. Scrape the dough out onto a lightly floured work surface and knead into a ball. Wrap in plastic and refrigerate while preparing the filling.

For best results, mix the filling by hand. Place the drained ricotta into a large mixing bowl and gently mix in the sugar with a rubber spatula, making sure not to beat the mixture which would liquefy it. Stir in remaining ingredients. Cover and chill.

To form the cannoli, divide the dough in half and roll 1 piece into a long strip, about 3 inches (8 cm) wide and about 18 inches (46 cm) long. Cut the dough into 3 inch (8 cm) circles and set aside. Repeat with the other half. Re-roll the scraps to make about 6 more disks of dough. Working with the first circles, roll over each one again and make it onto an oval about 5 inches (13 cm) long. Place one of the tubes on the dough lengthwise and gently pull one side of the dough around it without stretching. Moisten the top lightly with the egg white and pull the other side around to meet it. Press hard to seal. Repeat with the remaining circles.

To fry the cannoli shells, pour the oil into a 3 quart (2.75 l) pan or Dutch oven and heat it to 350°F (180°C). Fry the cannoli a few at a time, until they are a deep golden brown. Immediately slide the shells off the tubes by gripping one end of the cylinder with tongs and using a mitt-covered hand or paper towel, gently grip the shell and twist and pull at the same time. Cool the shells on absorbent paper.

Immediately before serving, fill the cannoli with the chilled cream, using a pastry bag with no tube on the end. Press chopped pistachios against the exposed cream and dust the cannoli lightly with the confectioners' sugar.

HINT   Use an accurate thermometer to measure the temperature of the frying oil. A good one looks like a ruler, not a disk with a stem attached.

FRIED PASTRIES ARE among the glories of the Italian dessert repertoire. They are often associated with Carnival, the season of feasting that precedes the fasting of Lent. Most fried pastries used to be fried in animal fat—forbidden during Lent—and this is how they came to be associated with Carnival. Cannoli are found all over Sicily, but these classic ricotta-filled ones are typical of Palermo. This recipe is based on those that I tasted at the Sant'Andrea convent in Palermo.

Please note: special metal tubes are needed for frying the cannoli. These are easy to find in kitchenware and department stores.

nick malgieri

Sicilian Fig-Filled "Bracelets"
Buccellati

THIS TRADITIONAL

Sicilian pastry filled with dried figs is made in many forms. Some are small shapes like cookies, though this recipe yields large rings meant to be cut or broken into pieces. The name means "bracelet" referring to their ring shape.

nick malgieri

MAKES TWO LARGE CAKES, EACH 8-10 INCHES (20-25 CM) IN DIAMETER

The Pasta Frolla
3¼ cups all-purpose flour
½ cup sugar
1 teaspoon baking powder
½ teaspoon salt
1¾ sticks (14 tablespoons) cold butter or lard
2 large eggs
¼ cup milk

The Fig Filling
3 cups (about 1 pound (450 g)) dried
   Calimyrna figs, stemmed and diced
⅔ cup dark raisins

⅔ cup toasted sliced almonds
4 ounces (115 g) semisweet chocolate,
   cut into ¼ inch (6 mm) pieces
⅓ cup apricot or other preserves
2 tablespoons dark rum
2 teaspoons instant espresso powder
1 teaspoon cinnamon
1 teaspoon ground cloves

The Egg Wash
1 egg
1 egg yolk
Pinch salt

METHOD   To make the pasta frolla dough, pulse the flour, sugar, salt and baking powder in a food processor fitted with the steel blade. Cut the butter into 12 pieces and add to the work bowl. Pulse about 15 times to mix in the butter finely. Whisk the eggs and milk together and add to the work bowl. Continue to pulse until the dough forms a ball. If the dough is dry and refuses to form a ball, add a couple of teaspoons of milk, a teaspoon at a time, until it does.

Spread a piece of plastic wrap on the work surface. Scrape the dough onto the plastic and form it into a square. Wrap and chill the dough while preparing the filling.

To make the filling, combine the filling ingredients in the work bowl of a food processor fitted with the steel blade. Pulse repeatedly until the ingredients are finely chopped, but not puréed. Pour the filling from the work bowl to a shallow bowl.

To make the egg wash, whisk all ingredients together in a bowl.

When you are ready to bake the buccellati, set racks in the upper and lower thirds of the oven and preheat to 350°F (180°C). Cover 2 baking sheets or jelly roll pans with parchment or foil.

To form the buccellati, remove the dough from the refrigerator and divide it in half. Place each half on a floured surface and knead briefly until the dough is smooth and malleable. Roll one piece to a 12 inch (30 cm) disk and slide it onto a cutting board or cookie sheet. Cut a 4 inch (10 cm) disk from the middle. Arrange half the filling in a ring between the outside edge of the dough and the center opening. Slash the dough on both sides around the filling with a paring knife or pizza wheel and wrap the dough around the filling to enclose it completely. Invert one of the lined

baking pans on the buccellato and pick up both pans with the pastry between and invert them. Remove the top pan and paint the buccellato with the egg wash, using a soft brush. Use a knife or scissors to slash or snip three rows of cuts on the buccellato: on top, inside and outside. Let the buccellato rest at room temperature while preparing the second one.

Bake the buccellati until the dough is baked through and they are a deep golden color, about 30-40 minutes. Halfway through the baking, switch racks so that the one on the bottom rack is on the top and vice versa. Also remember that if your oven gives strong bottom heat, bake the one on the bottom on a doubled pan (two pans stacked together) for better insulation. Cool the buccellati on the pans on racks.

Serve buccellati as a casual dessert, cutting them into slices at the table. To store the buccellati, double wrap them in plastic and keep in a tin or plastic container with a tight-fitting cover. They keep almost indefinitely.

Almond Cookies
Brutti-Boni

MAKES ABOUT 40 COOKIES

2 cups almonds
½ cup pine nuts
½ cup sugar

3 egg whites, lightly beaten with a fork
½ cup pastry flour

METHOD   Preheat the oven to 350°F (180°C). Line a baking sheet with parchment paper. Combine the almonds, pine nuts and sugar in a food processor and process until the mixture is the texture of coarse cornmeal. Pour into a bowl, add the egg whites and flour and mix until absorbed into a dough.

Roll the dough into balls slightly larger than a walnut and place on the prepared baking sheet 1 inch (2.5 cm) apart. Press the top lightly to flatten and pinch the sides so the cookie isn't quite round. Bake in the preheated oven until barely colored, about 12-15 minutes. Let cool before serving. The inside of the cookie will be tantalizingly moist.

MY FAVORITE VERSION of this simple almond cookie comes from the Tuscan bakery Mattei in Prato and is different from all others that I've ever encountered. They're called *brutti e buoni* or *brutti ma buoni*, ugly but tasty (although they're not really unattractive). Tuscan dialect turns them into *brutti-boni*. They're almost too easy to make.

faith willinger

Tuscan Almond Biscotti
Cantuccini

think of biscotti as the type of
cookies that are first baked as
a log, then sliced and re-baked,
the word refers to cookies in
general in Italian. These classic
Tuscan biscotti are seen all over
Italy. Though the cinnamon is
an optional flavoring, they are
always made with almonds.
Try hazelnuts or even walnuts
for a change of pace.

nick malgieri

MAKES ABOUT 6 DOZEN BISCOTTI

2 cups all-purpose flour
⅔ cup sugar
2 teaspoons baking powder
½ teaspoon cinnamon

¼ teaspoon salt
1⅔ cups whole unblanched almonds
3 large eggs

METHOD   Set a rack in the middle level of the oven and preheat to 350°F (180°C). Cover 2 baking sheets or jelly roll pans with parchment or foil.

In a large bowl stir together the dry ingredients, then stir in the almonds. Make a well in the center of the dry ingredients and add the eggs. Use a rubber spatula to beat the eggs to break them up, then gradually draw the dry ingredients into the liquid to make a stiff dough.

Scrape the dough to a lightly floured work surface and roll the dough under the palms of your hands to make a thick cylinder. Cut the dough in half and roll each again to a log about 12 inches (30 cm) long. Transfer the logs to one of the prepared pans spacing them well apart from each other and from the sides of the pan. Bake the logs until they are risen, spread and a deep golden color, about 30 minutes. Make sure they feel firm when pressed with a fingertip before removing them from the oven.

Slide the paper from the pan to a rack. Leave the oven on and reposition the racks to divide the oven in thirds.

After the logs have cooled completely use a sharp serrated knife to slice them every ⅓ inch (7 mm). Place the slices, cut-side-down, on the prepared pans. Bake the biscotti for about 15-20 minutes, or until they are a light golden color all over. Cool on a rack. Store the cooled biscotti in a tin or plastic container with a tight fitting cover.

HINT   Neatness and uniformity count for biscotti. Try to make cookies all the same size—they always look neater and more appetizing.

Tuscan Almond Biscotti (Cantuccini),
Sicilian "Twisted" Cookies (Infasciadedde),
and Venetian Cornmeal Cookies (Zaleti),
served with Grown-up Hot Chocolate.

Sicilian "Twisted" Cookies
Infasciadedde

THESE WERE A SPECIALTY

**of my late great-aunt, Elvira
Pescatore Basile, who made
them every Christmas.**

nick malgieri

MAKES ABOUT 48 COOKIES

1 recipe Pasta Frolla,
   medium batch (see page 151)
The Filling
1½ cups unblanched almonds
½ cup honey
½ teaspoon cinnamon

For Finishing
Honey
Toasted sliced almonds

METHOD   Prepare and chill the pasta frolla dough.

Set racks in the upper and lower thirds of the oven and preheat to 350°F (180°C). Cover 2 baking sheets or jelly roll pans with parchment or foil.

For the filling, grind the almonds in a food processor then add the honey and cinnamon. If mixture is very firm, add a tablespoon of water.

Divide the pasta frolla dough into 2 parts and roll each into a 12 inch (30 cm) square. Cut the dough into 8 strips, each 1½ x 12 inches (4 x 30 cm). Spread the filling down the center of each strip, then fold the strip up to contain the filling. Cut into 4 inch (10 cm) lengths and twist once or twice. Repeat with the second piece of dough. Bake the cookies until they are pale and golden, about 12-15 minutes. Remember to alternate the pans from one rack to the other and to double the pan on the bottom (stack 2 pans together) if your oven gives strong bottom heat.

Before serving, drizzle with the honey and sprinkle with the almonds.

Venetian Cornmeal Cookies
Zaleti

MAKES ABOUT 6 DOZEN SMALL COOKIES

1¼ cups yellow cornmeal
1¼ cups unbleached all-purpose flour
⅓ cup sugar
¼ teaspoon salt
1 teaspoon baking powder
10 tablespoons (1¼ sticks) cold unsalted
    butter, cut into 12 pieces

¾ cup currants or raisins
1 large egg
1 large egg yolk
2 teaspoons vanilla extract
Confectioners' sugar, for dusting

METHOD   Set racks in the upper and lower thirds of the oven and preheat to 350°F (180°C). Cover 2 baking sheets or jelly roll pans with parchment or foil.

In a large bowl combine the cornmeal, flour, sugar, salt and baking powder. Add the butter and rub between the palms of your hands as for a pastry dough, continuing to rub until the butter is mixed in fairly finely, but the mixture is still powdery. Stir in the currants. Whisk together the egg, yolk and vanilla and add to the dough. Stir the liquid in with a fork until the mixture leaves the sides of the bowl and forms a soft dough.

Scrape the dough out onto a floured work surface and roll it under the palms of your hands to a fat cylinder. Cut the dough into 3 pieces and roll each to a cylinder 12 inches (30 cm) long. Flatten slightly with the palm of your hand and cut each into ½ inch (1.5 cm) thick slices on the diagonal to form diamond shapes. Place the cookies on the prepared pans leaving about 1 inch (2.5 cm) all around each.

Bake the cookies until they are well risen and firm, about 20 minutes. Halfway through the baking, switch racks so that the one on the bottom rack is on the top and vice versa. Also remember that if your oven gives strong bottom heat, bake the one on the bottom on a doubled pan (2 pans stacked together) for better insulation.

Cool the zaleti on the pans on racks. Just before serving, dust lightly with confectioners' sugar.

Store the zaleti in a tin.

THESE CORNMEAL COOKIES are popular in the Veneto. The name means "little yellow things" and the cookie is seen in one form or another throughout Northeastern Italy. There are primitive versions of zaleti that are made from sweetened baked polenta; this one is considerably more delicate.

nick malgieri

Chocolate Almond Honey Cookies
Mostaccioli

MAKES ABOUT 30 COOKIES

The Dough
1⅔ cups all-purpose flour
⅓ cup unsweetened cocoa powder,
     sifted after measuring
½ cup sugar
¾ cup ground almonds
½ teaspoon cinnamon

½ teaspoon cloves
½ teaspoon baking soda
⅓ cup honey
⅓ cup red wine
The Icing
2 cups confectioners' sugar
3 tablespoons water

METHOD   Set racks in the upper and lower thirds of the oven and preheat to 350°F (180°C). Cover 2 baking sheets or jelly roll pans with parchment or foil.

For the dough, in a large bowl combine all the ingredients except the honey and wine; stir well to mix. In another small bowl, stir the honey and wine together then use a rubber spatula to stir the liquid into the dry ingredients. Continue stirring until the mixture forms a soft dough.

Scrape the dough out onto a floured work surface and roll it under the palms of your hands to a fat cylinder. Cut the dough into 4 pieces and roll each to a cylinder 12 inches (30 cm) long. Flatten slightly with the palm of your hand and cut each into diamond shapes. Place the cookies on the prepared pans leaving about an inch (2.5 cm) all around each. Bake the cookies until they are well risen and firm, about 20 minutes. Halfway through the baking, switch racks so that the one on the bottom rack is on the top and vice versa. Also remember that if your oven gives strong bottom heat, bake the one on the bottom on a doubled pan (2 pans stacked together) for better insulation. Cool the mostaccioli on the pans on racks.

To make the icing, combine the confectioners' sugar and water in a small pan and stir well to mix with a small wooden spoon. Place over low heat and cook, stirring occasionally, until the icing is just simmering around the sides of the pan. Remove from the heat and quickly brush the warm icing on the cooled cookies. Let the cookies stay on the pans until the icing is dry.

Store the mostaccioli in a tin.

Sweet Easter Ring Cookies
Taralli Dolci di Pasqua

MAKES ABOUT 20 COOKIES

The Dough

3 cups all-purpose flour

4 teaspoons baking powder

3 eggs

½ cup sugar

6 tablespoons (¾ stick) unsalted butter, melted

1 tablespoon vanilla extract

The Icing

2 cups confectioners' sugar

2 tablespoons water

1 tablespoon lemon juice

1 teaspoon vanilla extract

Multi-colored nonpareils, optional

METHOD Set racks in the upper and lower third of your oven and preheat to 350°F (180°C). Cover 2 baking sheets or jelly roll pans with parchment paper.

For the dough, combine the flour and baking powder in a small bowl, stirring well to mix. In another large bowl, whisk the eggs, then whisk in all the remaining ingredients in order, except the nonpareils. Fold in the flour mixture. Turn the dough out on a floured surface and knead lightly to mix. Separate into 20 equal pieces. Roll each into an 8 inch (20 cm) rope, then into a circle. Place 6 or 8 on each prepared pan. Bake the taralli until they are well puffed and deep golden, about 25 to 30 minutes. Halfway through the baking, switch racks so that the pan on the bottom rack is on the top and vice versa. Also remember that if your oven gives strong bottom heat, bake the taralli on the bottom on a doubled pan (two pans stacked together) for better insulation. Cool on racks.

For the icing, combine all ingredients in a saucepan and heat gently until lukewarm. Brush over the tops of the cooled cookies. Sprinkle with the multi-colored nonpareils, if desired. Store the taralli in a tin.

Chocolate Gelato with Sour Cherries and Whipped Cream

THE *ARLECCHINO*, OR

"harlequin," is a classic Italian

gelato combo—chocolate ice

cream, candied cherries and

whipped cream.

faith willinger

SERVES 4

1 pint (500ml) chocolate ice cream

8 tablespoons candied sour cherries

8 tablespoons lightly sweetened whipped cream

METHOD About 30 minutes before serving, remove the ice cream from the freezer and place in the refrigerator for 20 minutes to soften. To serve, place a large scoop or two of the softened ice cream in 4 individual bowls. Top each with 2 tablespoons of the cherries and a dollop of the whipped cream.

Banana Gelato
Gelato di Banana

FRUIT, WATER AND SUGAR

are gently frozen and the

results are magic. It's strange

but true that this gelato

doesn't have any fat whatsoev-

er, although it never set out to

be a low-fat recipe. Most

Italian fruit-flavored gelato is

actually sorbetto, or what

some people might call sorbet.

faith willinger

MAKES ABOUT 1 QUART (1 L). SERVES 4 TO 6

1 cup minus 2 tablespoons sugar

1 cup bottled or filtered water

1½ pounds (750 g) ripe bananas

2 tablespoons lemon juice

1 teaspoon egg white, lightly beaten with a fork

METHOD In a small saucepan set over medium heat, cook the sugar and water, stirring, until the sugar has dissolved. Remove from the heat and let cool.

In a food processor or blender, purée the bananas until smooth. Transfer 2 cups to a medium bowl, stir in the lemon juice and cooled sugar syrup and chill for at least 1 hour or up to a day. Stir in the egg white, transfer to an ice cream machine and freeze according to directions. Remove the gelato from the machine and eat immediately or transfer to a quart container, cover and freeze for no longer than 3 hours, or optimum consistency will be lost.

Chocolate Gelato with Sour Cherries and Whipped Cream

Orange Slices with Vanilla Gelato and Balsamic Vinegar

SERVES 4

1 pint (500 ml) vanilla ice cream
4 large oranges, peeled and thinly sliced
About 4 tablespoons aged balsamic vinegar

METHOD About 30 minutes before serving, remove the ice cream from the freezer and place in the refrigerator for about 20 minutes to soften. To serve, divide the orange slices among 4 individual bowls. Top each with a scoop of the softened ice cream and a tablespoon-drizzle of the balsamic vinegar. Or substitute a drizzle of honey.

HINT If you don't have aged balsamic vinegar, pour ¼ cup industrial balsamic vinegar into a small saucepan and cook over high heat until it reduces by half. Remove from the heat and stir in 1 tablespoon industrial balsamic vinegar and cool.

STORE-BOUGHT ICE CREAM is fancied up with a drizzle of balsamic vinegar and decorated with a few orange slices—a grown-up version of the orange popsicle.

faith willinger

Custard Gelato
Gelato di Crema

SERVES 4 TO 6

2¼ cups whole milk
⅓ cup heavy whipping ceam
¾ cup, minus 1 tablespoon sugar

1 (3 inch) (8 cm) strip lemon zest, optional
5 egg yolks

METHOD In a medium saucepan, scald the milk and cream with half the sugar and the lemon zest, if using, stirring until the sugar is dissolved. Set aside. In a medium bowl, beat the egg yolks with the remaining sugar until thick and pale. Slowly beat the hot milk mixture into the egg yolks, then transfer the mixture to the top of a double boiler. Cook over low heat, stirring constantly, until the mixture thickens slightly at a temperature of 170°F (76°C). Be careful not to let the mixture boil.

Pour the custard through a sieve into a metal bowl. Place the bowl over water and ice in a larger bowl to cool quickly. Cover with plastic wrap and refrigerate for at least 6 hours. Transfer to an ice cream machine and freeze according to the directions. Serve the gelato immediately or transfer to a quart container, cover and place in the freezer for no longer than 3 hours, or optimum consistency will be lost.

THIS IS A CLASSIC custard gelato: milk enriched with plenty of egg yolks, called "reds" in Italy for their intense reddish-orange color. Quality eggs will yield the best results.

faith willinger

Orange Slices with Vanilla Gelato and Balsamic Vinegar

Peaches with White Wine

I LEARNED TO MARINATE

peaches with white wine in

Rome, when I worked in a

restaurant to learn about

Roman cooking. Use more

sugar if you want to be

really Italian!

faith willinger

SERVES 2

1 pound (450 g) ripe peaches, preferably
   in season
Juice of ½ lemon

2-3 tablespoons sugar
½ cup white wine

METHOD   Peel and pit the peaches. Slice thinly and transfer to a large bowl.
Sprinkle with the lemon juice, sugar and wine, stir well and let marinate for at
least 10 minutes. Lengthy soaking results in soggy fruit. Serve immediately.

Strawberries with Red Wine

ONE OF THE EASIEST

recipes I know, and one

of my favorites during

the short but wonderful

strawberry season.

faith willinger

SERVES 2

1 pint (500 ml) ripe strawberries,
   preferably local and in season
Juice of ½ lemon

3-4 tablespoons sugar
½ cup good quality red wine

METHOD   Clean the berries well. Cut off the leaves, cut in half and transfer to a
small bowl. Sprinkle with the lemon juice, sugar and wine, stir and let marinate for
at least 10 minutes. Lengthy soaking will result in soggy berries. Serve immediately.

Peaches with White Wine

Pears and Prunes with Wine and Spice

dessert, simple to prepare
and dramatic looking on a
platter. Those who want a
fancier dessert can serve it
with sweetened mascarpone
or ricotta.

faith willinger

SERVES 4 TO 6

4-6 firm pears
3-4 cups red wine
½ cup sugar

2 strips lemon zest
1 stick cinnamon (optional)
1 cup prunes, with or without pits

METHOD   Peel the pears with a potato peeler, leaving the stem as a handle. Slice off the bottom end so that the pear stands up. Place the pears in a heavy-bottomed non-reactive pan just large enough to hold them. Use a pot with a tight-fitting lid that will fit easily over the pears.

Pour the wine over the pears, add the reaming ingredients, and bring to a boil over high heat. Reduce the heat to its lowest setting, cover and cook until tender when poked with a knife, about 15-25 minutes.

Using a slotted spoon, transfer the pears and prunes to a serving dish. Raise the heat to high and reduce the wine syrup until lightly thickened, about 15-20 minutes. Serve at room temperature, plain or with *Custard Gelato* (see page 185).

Pears and Prunes with Wine and Spice

Roasted Strawberries with Balsamic Vinegar and Cinnamon Sticks

SERVES 4 TO 6

2 pints (1 l) strawberries, hulled and quartered

1 tablespoon balsamic vinegar

¼ cup dark brown sugar

2 tablespoons unsalted butter

3 cinnamon sticks

METHOD   Preheat the oven to 450°F (230°C). Put all of the ingredients in an oven-proof baking dish and cook until the berries have softened and the sauce is slightly reduced, about 6-10 minutes, stirring occasionally. Remove from the oven and serve. It is delicious over vanilla gelato or angel food cake.

OKAY, I KNOW THAT THE idea of cooking strawberries may seem strange—especially with balsamic vinegar! But let me assure you that you will love the results. The Italians will drizzle balsamic vinegar over many fruits and berries and this takes that practice one step further. This is a wonderful way to use strawberries that are not perfect. Please be sure to discard the cinnamon sticks before serving.

joe simone

Roasted Strawberries with Balsamic Vinegar and Cinnamon Sticks

Gorgonzola with Honey

EASIER THAN SLICED

bread—and a great way to use up honey, which seems to multiply in my cupboard at home.

faith willinger

SERVES 2

4-8 ounces (115-225 g) Gorgonzola cheese
2-3 tablespoons honey, preferably chestnut

METHOD   Place a slice of the Gorgonzola on each serving plate and top with a drizzle of honey.

Grown-up Hot Chocolate

THIS SICILIAN VERSION

of hot chocolate has no milk and relies on first rate bittersweet chocolate and a dollop of whipped cream for greatest success.

faith willinger

SERVES 1

3-4 ounces (90-115 g) bittersweet chocolate, use the finest quality available
1 cup water
2-3 tablespoons unsweetened whipping cream

METHOD   In the top of a double boiler over boiling water, pour in the water and add the chocolate. Cook until melted. Pour into a blender and whip for 30 seconds, or use an immersion mixer. Return the mixture to the double boiler and heat to the desired temperature. Pour into a large cup and top with the whipped cream.

Gorgonzola with Honey

HAZELNUTS, ALSO SOME-

times called filberts, are a

wonderful way to set off the

slightly acid flavors of young

goat cheese.

nancy harmon jenkins

Toasted Hazelnut Goat Cheese with Honey-Orange Sauce

SERVES 6

1 cup toasted hazelnuts (see HINT)
1 pound (450 g) cylinder of fresh young
    goat cheese
½ cup honey, preferably flowery

½ cup extra-virgin olive oil
1 tablespoon grated orange zest
1 tablespoon freshly squeezed orange juice

METHOD   Pulse the hazelnuts in a food processor until they are as fine as bread-crumbs. Spread the ground hazelnuts on a plate. Cut the goat cheese into rounds about 1 inch (2.5 cm) thick. Dip each round—top, bottom and sides—into the hazel-nuts to coat thoroughly. Arrange 2 rounds on each of 6 dessert plates. Set the dessert plates in the refrigerator.

In a small saucepan set over low heat, warm the honey, olive oil, orange zest and orange juice, stirring occasionally. The mixture should be very hot but not boil-ing. When ready to serve, remove the plates from the refrigerator, spoon over the hot sauce and serve immediately.

HINT   To toast the hazelnuts, preheat the oven to 350°F (180°C). Spread the hazel-nuts on a baking sheet and bake for 10-15 minutes, or until they are golden brown. Transfer the nuts to a kitchen towel and rub vigorously to get rid of as much of the outside skin as possible.

Toasted Hazelnut Goat Cheese with Honey-Orange Sauce

Index

(Page numbers in *italics* refer to illustrations.)